I0817608

MODERN STARS

TIMOTHÉE CHALAMET

by Tammy Gagne

Essential Library

An Imprint of Abdo Publishing

abdobooks.com

ABDOBOOKS.COM

Published by Abdo Publishing, a division of ABDO, PO Box 398166, Minneapolis, Minnesota 55439.

Printed in China.
102025
012026

Cover Photo: Gilbert Flores/Golden Globes 2024/Getty Images Entertainment/Getty Images
Interior Photos: Neilson Barnard/Getty Images Entertainment/Getty Images, 5; Kevin Mazur/WireImage/Getty Images, 6; John Phillips/Getty Images for BFI/Getty Images Entertainment/Getty Images, 9; Roberto Machado Noa/LightRocket/Getty Images, 11; Raymond Boyd/Michael Ochs Archives/Getty Images, 15; Allen Berezovsky/Getty Images Sport/Getty Images, 16; Kevork Djansezian/Getty Images Entertainment/Getty Images, 18; Gotham/GC Images/Getty Images, 20; Shutterstock Images, 21; Guy Christian/Hemis.fr/Alamy, 22; Ajay Suresh/Flickr, 27; Pascal Le Segretain/Getty Images Entertainment/Getty Images, 31; James Devaney/Getty Images Entertainment/Getty Images, 32; Alexi Rosenfeld/Getty Images Entertainment/Getty Images, 34; Fox 21/Album/Alamy, 36; Jason Kempin/Getty Images for Paramount Pictures International/Getty Images Entertainment/Getty Images, 39; Raymond Hall/GC Images/Getty Images, 40; Frazer Harrison/Getty Images Entertainment/Getty Images, 43; Daniel Zuchnik/Getty Images Entertainment/Getty Images, 46; Warner Brothers/Archive Photos/Moviepix/Getty Images, 47; Michael Buckner/Variety/Penske Media/Getty Images, 49; Phillip Faraone/Getty Images Entertainment/Getty Images, 51; Frenesy Film Company/La Cinéfacture/RT Features/Water's End/Album/Alamy, 53; Lorey Sebastian/Photo 12/Waypoint Entertainment/Grisbi Productions/Alamy, 56; Lifestyle Pictures/Alamy, 58; James Devaney/GC Images/Getty Images, 61; Photo 12/Netflix/Alamy, 63; Stephane Cardinale/Corbis Entertainment/Getty Images, 65; Desiree Navarro/Getty Images Entertainment/Getty Images, 66; Wilson Webb/Photo 12/7e Art/Columbia Pictures/Alamy, 70; Roger Do Minh/Photo 12/Searchlight Pictures/Alamy, 72; Legendary Entertainment/Warner Bros./Album/Alamy, 75; Chiabella James/Legendary Entertainment/Warner Bros./Album/Alamy, 76; Warner Bros./Album/Alamy, 79; Frenesy Film Company/Per Capita Productions/Album/Alamy, 83; The Chosunilbo JNS/ImaZins/Getty Images, 84; Elisabetta A. Villa/Getty Images Entertainment/Getty Images, 87; Jose Perez/Bauer-Griffin/GC Images/Getty Images, 89, 96; Bettmann/Getty Images, 91; Photo 12/Searchlight Pictures/Alamy, 93; Jeff Kravitz/FilmMagic, Inc./Getty Images, 99

Editor: Kari Cornell
Series Designer: Karli Hughes

Library of Congress Control Number: 2025939311

PUBLISHER'S CATALOGING-IN-PUBLICATION DATA

Names: Gagne, Tammy, author.
Title: Timothée Chalamet / by Tammy Gagne
Description: Minneapolis, Minnesota: Abdo Publishing, 2026 | Series: Modern stars | Includes online resources and index.
Identifiers: ISBN 9781098298128 (lib. bdg.) | ISBN 9798384931928 (ebook)
Subjects: LCSH: Chalamet, Timothée--Juvenile literature. | Actors--United States--Biography--Juvenile literature. | Motion picture actors and actresses--United States--Biography--Juvenile literature. | Television actors and actresses--United States--Biography--Juvenile literature.
Classification: DDC 791.4302--dc23

CONTENTS

Chapter 1
A NIGHT TO REMEMBER 4

Chapter 2
CREATIVE BEGINNINGS.................... 14

Chapter 3
A STAR IN THE MAKING.................... 26

Chapter 4
PROGRESS AND CHALLENGES 38

Chapter 5
THE YEAR THAT CHANGED HIS CAREER 50

Chapter 6
SHOWING HIS RANGE.................... 62

Chapter 7
FROM INDIE FILMS TO BLOCKBUSTERS.................... 74

Chapter 8
LIKE A ROLLING STONE.................... 88

Essential Facts 100
Glossary 102
Additional Resources 104
Source Notes 106
Index 110
About the Author 112

CHAPTER ONE

A NIGHT TO REMEMBER

Timothée Chalamet arrived at the 2018 Academy Awards dressed in an all-white tuxedo. Although he had been acting for years, this was the 22-year-old's first time at the Oscars. He could hardly believe he was a contender for one of the night's highly coveted statues.

Nominated for his role in the 2017 film *Call Me by Your Name*, Chalamet brought his mother, Nicole Flender, as his date to the ceremony. When red carpet host Michael Strahan stopped them for a quick interview, Flender shared how proud she was of the wonderful job her son had done in the popular film. The movie, which is set in Italy, tells the story of a

Timothée Chalamet walked the red carpet with his mom, Nicole Flender, at the 2018 Academy Awards. >>

At the 2018 Academy Awards, Chalamet talked with many actors he had long admired, including Matthew McConaughey.

teenager named Elio Perlman, played by Chalamet. Elio experiences his first love while spending the summer at his family's villa in Lombardy, Italy.

Chalamet was the youngest person to be nominated for Best Actor at the Academy Awards, often called the Oscars, in almost 80 years. Oscars host Jimmy Kimmel joked about Chalamet's age in his opening monologue. Kimmel said, "Timothée is missing *Paw Patrol* to be here tonight."[1] The young actor laughed along with the rest of the audience.

IN GOOD COMPANY

Chalamet was enamored by the stars around him at the Oscars ceremony. He was used to watching these actors on the big screen. Now, he sat among them in the audience. He later said that above all else, he was a movie fan. Although he admitted that he felt starstruck, he didn't seem embarrassed by it.

The young actor appeared both humble and confident. In an interview, Chalamet said, "It's nuts. I mean, I'm just trying not to pinch myself."[2] Sometimes Chalamet felt as if he might be dreaming about his acting success. The possibility of winning the Oscar was just part of the joy he felt. He was also proud to have been part of the acclaimed *Call Me by Your Name*. Acting was already much more than a job to Chalamet, and being nominated for an Academy Award was a big honor.

Four other people were nominated for the Best Actor award, giving Chalamet serious competition for the Oscar.

AN HONOR JUST TO BE NOMINATED

When a competitor wins an award, actors sometimes say it was an honor just to be nominated. In the case of an Oscar, however, being nominated truly is a significant form of recognition. Many actors value the nomination in large part because it comes from their peers. Members of the Academy of Motion Picture Arts and Sciences' Actors Branch vote to determine the Oscar nominees each year. When the time comes to vote for the winner, all academy members cast ballots. These members include actors, writers, directors, costume designers, makeup artists, producers, and other professionals in the film industry.

He was up against Daniel Day-Lewis for *Phantom Thread*, Daniel Kaluuya for *Get Out*, Denzel Washington for *Roman J. Israel, Esq.*, and Gary Oldman for *Darkest Hour*. Day-Lewis had been nominated five other times, winning three of the Oscars. Washington had been nominated for Best Actor five other times, winning once. Oldman had been nominated one other time but hadn't yet taken home the trophy.

When the award for Best Actor was announced, Oldman won the Oscar. Chalamet's fans had wanted him to win, but they took joy from his nomination at such a young age. Oldman also saw Chalamet's nomination as something to celebrate. He spoke highly of the younger actor after the Oscars ceremony.

"I'm thrilled for Chalamet," he said. "He's a lovely kid, I mean, really, he's a kid and he's a charmer. Hugely talented. I said to him tonight in the words of Arnold [Schwarzenegger], 'You'll be back.' This is probably it for me. He's got years."[3]

FOR THE WIN

Although Chalamet didn't take home the Oscar in 2018, he did win several other awards for his performance in *Call Me by Your Name*. These awards included the New York Film Critics Circle Award, the London Film Critics' Circle Award, and the Independent Spirit Award. James Ivory also won the Academy Award for Best Adapted Screenplay for the film.

Chalamet attended the premiere of *Call Me by Your Name* with costars, *from left*, Armie Hammer, Ester Garrel, and director Luca Guadagnino on October 9, 2017.

A CAREER-CHANGING MOMENT

Being nominated for an Oscar is a huge accomplishment for an actor of any age. Many people consider the Academy Award the most prestigious honor in the film industry. Oscar nominations also make movies more popular with ticket buyers, which translates to more revenue for the films. A movie does not need to win to benefit in this way. The attention from a nomination can make a big difference for independent films such as *Call Me by Your Name*, which are generally shown in fewer theaters than big-budget productions are.

Chalamet doesn't act for money or fame. He said, "The idea has been to tell good stories with good filmmakers."[4] Achieving this goal becomes easier after being nominated for an Academy Award. Oscar nominees gain more attention from casting directors, film producers, and moviegoing audiences. After being nominated for an Oscar, many actors suddenly begin receiving more scripts from movie producers than they have time to read. Instead of competing for roles, they often have their choice of many projects.

> **"The joyous part of this experience was getting to shoot the film. That was all that was expected when we signed [on] the dotted line. . . . These are cherries, cherries, cherries, cherries on top."**[5]
>
> —Timothée Chalamet on *Call Me by Your Name*'s four Oscar nominations

A DIFFERENT KIND OF LEADING MAN

Since 2017, Chalamet has become one of the most popular stars in the entertainment industry. While movies are his primary medium, he also has a range of other talents. Chalamet has hosted *Saturday Night Live* three times, with his first appearance coming in 2020. In 2021, he starred in a Super Bowl commercial for Cadillac. He can also sing and play several instruments.

Chalamet has hosted *Saturday Night Live*, filmed at 30 Rockefeller Plaza in Midtown Manhattan, three times. Hosting has been known to give a boost to celebrity careers.

Having grown up in a family that includes dancers, writers, and a film director, Chalamet is no stranger to the arts. He has a genuine love of movies, theater, music, and dance as both a performer and a spectator. Some people even call the young star an *artthrob*, meaning a cross between an artist and a heartthrob.

While many young male actors build their muscles to take on traditionally masculine roles, Chalamet embraces his slender physique and emotional vulnerability. Since his rise to fame, he has shown that strong characters do not always have to be physically imposing. He played a rebellious monarch in *The King*, a charming dreamer in

Wonka, and a warrior who experiences prophetic visions in the *Dune* films. He does not match the typical appearance or personality of a leading man, yet his name is atop the credits of some of the biggest blockbuster films of the 2020s.

CHALAMET'S STYLE

When Chalamet is acting, he wears clothing chosen by costume designers. When he isn't playing a character, though, he is known for making some bold fashion choices. He often arrives at award shows and other events in eye-catching ensembles. In 2018, he donned a black suit with a red floral pattern for the Toronto, Canada, premiere of *Beautiful Boy*. For the Venice, Italy, premiere of *Bones and All* in 2022, he wore a sleeveless and backless red shirt with red pants.

Chalamet's early experiences in musical theater helped him develop his talents for singing and dancing. The actor has applied his dancing and musical talents to several of his film characters. He performs a classic jazz song called "Everything Happens to Me" as Gatsby Welles in *A Rainy Day in New York*. In *Wonka*, he sings and dances in several musical numbers. Although Elio does not sing in *Call Me by Your Name*, the character does dance at a party. The scene helps show the audience the character's awkward yet uninhibited personality.

In 2024, Chalamet appeared in another movie in which he used his musical talent. This time, he was playing a real-life person, folk singer Bob Dylan, in the biopic

A Complete Unknown. Chalamet received widespread praise for his portrayal of Dylan. The actor bears a remarkable resemblance to the singer as a young man, and he sounds a lot like the music icon as well. Chalamet sings several of Dylan's best-known songs in the film.

Gary Oldman ended up being right about the young actor getting another shot at an Academy Award. On January 23, 2025, Chalamet received his second Academy Award nomination for Best Actor for his portrayal of Dylan. While he didn't win, it was clear that Chalamet had become recognized as one of Hollywood's most talented and popular stars.

CHAPTER TWO

CREATIVE BEGINNINGS

Timothée Hal Chalamet was born on December 27, 1995, in New York City. *Timothée* is the French version of the name *Timothy*. Chalamet's parents used this spelling because his father is French. The name is pronounced differently too. As Timothée told Jimmy Kimmel, "Honestly, it's 'Tim-oh-tay,' but I would not oblige you to say it like that."[1] Most of his friends call him Timmy.

His father, Marc Chalamet, is a journalist. Marc met his wife, Nicole Flender, while on a business trip to New York City. He worked for the Associated Press in Paris, France, before starting his own news agency, News of America, in 1987. He has also worked

Timothée's family lived at Manhattan Plaza, a high-rise apartment building located in Midtown Manhattan, when he was growing up. >>

Timothée and his father, Marc Chalamet, attended an NBA Los Angeles Lakers–Boston Celtics game in 2023.

on publications for the United Nations International Children's Fund (UNICEF) and as an editor for the United Nations. In 2019, he became the New York correspondent for *Le Parisien*, a well-known newspaper in France.

Flender shares her son's love of the arts. One might even say the arts are in their blood. Her brother, Rodman, is a film and television director. Flender's father, Harold, was a novelist and a screenwriter. Enid, Flender's mother, danced on Broadway professionally. Flender herself studied dance and performed with the New York City Ballet as a child.

She earned a ballet scholarship to attend Yale University but then moved to musical theater instead. She later appeared in several Broadway musicals, including *Fiddler on the Roof* and *Hello Dolly*. She eventually left show business to become a real estate agent in New York.

Timothée's only sibling is his sister, Pauline, who is three years older. Their mother encouraged them both to appreciate the arts from a young age. They attended many plays and musicals together, which she now thinks had a significant effect on her children's personalities and career choices. Timothée's favorite production was called *Slava's Snowshow*, which combined a traditional clown show with stunning visual effects. Pauline's favorite production was *Hair*, a musical about 1960s counterculture.

Pauline studied ballet and later began acting. Timothée was also interested in acting. Flender never pushed her kids toward performing, though. She said, "I planted seeds, and our lifestyle really inspired those interests, but they always had control of their careers. I was encouraging, but I wasn't like, 'You better get this job.'"[2]

Flender drove her kids to auditions, served as a chaperone on sets, and helped with financial tasks such

A CITIZEN OF TWO NATIONS

Both Timothée and his sister were born in the United States, but they have dual US and French citizenship. They were able to become citizens of the European nation because their father is a French citizen. French law grants citizenship by descent, meaning parents who are citizens can pass citizenship on to their children.

as paying taxes on the money they made. She also supported them by getting involved in the Actors' Equity Association. This labor union works to improve working conditions for actors. Flender feels strongly that child actors need to balance their work with their education. As part of the union, she lobbied for changes such as mandatory tutoring during workdays and fair wages for young performers.

Marc was hesitant about his children's involvement in show business. He wanted them to have normal lives as young people. Nonetheless, he didn't stand in the way of his kids pursuing their respective careers. Both he and their mother were supportive. Timothée said, "I think the most precious thing I get from my parents . . . is their love and support."[3]

A FAMILY OF STORYTELLERS

When Timothée and his sister were growing up, the Chalamet family lived in a high-rise apartment building

Timothée's older sister, Pauline, also acts professionally. The siblings attended the 90th Annual Academy Awards Governors Ball after the Oscars in March 2018.

called Manhattan Plaza. Many of their neighbors were actors, musicians, and other types of artists. This building and many others in the neighborhood were part of the Mitchell-Lama Housing Program, which provided affordable apartments to New Yorkers. Although the program is not restricted to people pursuing careers in show business, the reasonable rents attract many artists because New York is both an artistic hub and one of the most expensive places to live in the United States.

The Chalamets often heard music and melodic voices through the walls as people in the other apartments

Chalamet, a native New Yorker, is sometimes spotted around town.

practiced playing instruments and singing. Artists who have called the building home through the years include actor Robert De Niro, musician Alicia Keys, and playwright Tennessee Williams. Timothée's maternal grandmother lived in one of the apartments as well.

Growing up in such an environment might be thought to increase the appeal of performing. But for Chalamet it had a different effect. He said, "This building truthfully made me scared of acting because it's a tough lifestyle and a lot of people aren't doing fantastically. It actually terrified me."[4]

His parents' dynamic careers, however, showed him the value of good storytelling. The Chalamet kids grew up understanding the importance of having a global perspective. This was largely due to their father's job reporting on current events, politics, and the economy. In addition to her dancing and her career in real estate, Flender is also a writer.

She has penned articles for newspapers such as the *Boston Herald* about her experiences in the arts. She also wrote a book titled *Cool Careers Without College for People Who Love Movement*. Telling stories in creative ways appealed to young Timothée as well.

Chalamet's grandfather, Hal Flender, earned his master's degree from Columbia University, where he later taught film writing.

Summer trips to Le Chambon-sur-Lignon to visit family gave the Chalamets a break from city life.

Timothée never met his maternal grandfather, who was the source of his middle name and, some say, his appearance. Hal Flender died in 1975, but his life's work was steeped in storytelling. His novel *Paris Blues* was among his most successful works. It was adapted into a film starring Paul Newman and Sidney Poitier in 1961.

Hal also worked as a journalist, a TV writer, and a screenwriting teacher at several colleges, including

Columbia University. He instilled a love of reading in his daughter, who passed this love on to her own children. One of Timothée's favorite books as a child was George Orwell's *1984*, the classic novel about a government that oppressively controls its citizens.

SUMMERS IN FRANCE

Chalamet lived in the United States for most of his childhood. But he spent summer vacations in Le Chambon-sur-Lignon. This is a small village near the French city of Leon where his father grew up.

The visits allowed Timothée to spend time with his paternal grandparents, Roger and Jean Chalamet. Timothée's grandfather was a pastor, and his grandmother taught the French language to missionaries as they prepared to travel to Africa. Timothée often played outside while his parents and grandparents drank coffee and talked.

IN A DIFFERENT LEAGUE

Like many kids, Timothée once dreamed of becoming a professional soccer player. He grew up playing the sport in school. One of his teammates was Alex Muyl, whom Timothée describes as the most talented player he knew. Muyl went on to a professional career in the sport, joining the Nashville SC of Major League Soccer (MLS). As a teenager, Timothée coached younger kids when he visited France, where soccer is known as football. He remains a big fan of AS Saint-Étienne, one of France's most successful teams.

The time in France also gave Timothée the chance to spend time with his French cousins in a place that was the complete opposite of New York City. As a child, Timothée was bothered by many of the loud noises of the city, such as police sirens, car alarms, and traffic. The French countryside was entirely different. There, he could spend time exploring and playing outdoors while enjoying the more soothing sounds of streams and birds singing in the forest.

The Chalamet family often spoke French, both in France and back in the United States. French was Timothée's father's native language, and his mother had studied French in college. Spending so much time with his extended family in France helped him learn to speak the language especially well. Both he and his sister are fluent speakers. He has said that he sometimes even dreams in French.

MIXING ACTING AND MUSIC

Timothée took piano lessons through his early teen years. Music didn't draw him in as acting did, but some of the roles he has played required him to play instruments. Timothée didn't hesitate to learn the skills. He took six months of piano lessons when he was cast in *Call Me by Your Name*. He learned to play the guitar for the movie as well.

HIS FIRST STEPS INTO ACTING

When he was young, Timothée decided to go after small acting roles. His first dramatic television part was on the crime television show *Law & Order* in 2009 when he was 12. He had only a few lines of dialogue before his character, the murder victim of the episode, was killed. Timothée has called the television series "the mothership" of the acting community, as many successful actors have gotten their start on the long-running show.[5] Appearing on the show led to more work for him as well.

Timothée soon landed other jobs, including TV commercials. He has said that these jobs didn't offer much experience. He describes the work as "smile-as-big-as-you-can acting," but it was experience nonetheless.[6] It added to his short résumé and put some money in his pocket.

This was just the beginning for Timothée. His eighth-grade class at Booker T. Washington Middle School had voted him "Most Likely to Be Famous" in the school's yearbook. He still had high school and many big decisions ahead of him, but he was on a path that would lead him to big opportunities.

CHAPTER THREE

A STAR IN THE MAKING

Timothée attended Fiorello H. LaGuardia High School of Music & Art and Performing Arts. Both his sister and his mother had also gone to the school, which has several famous alumni in show business. Other performers who attended the school include actors Adrien Brody and Jennifer Aniston and rapper Nicki Minaj. Although LaGuardia is a public school, students must audition to get in, and the competition is fierce. The fact that Timothée's mother and sister attended the school did not pave the way for his entry.

Harry Shifman was the drama teacher at the school when Timothée and about 200 other students auditioned in 2009.[1] Timothée got a callback audition,

LaGuardia High School on Manhattan's Upper West Side has a long list of famous alumni. >>

ONE WAY
W 65 St
FIORELLO H. LA GUARDIA HIGH SCHOOL
OF MUSIC & ART AND PERFORMING ARTS

in which he performed two monologues and one scene for Shifman. The teacher noticed something different about Timothée right away.

Shifman recalls, "I do remember going, 'Who is this?' Either a kid really connects emotionally . . . or a kid's got style and flare and can use their voice and face. It's rare to see a kid at that age who has both of those things happening."[2] Shifman saw these talents in Timothée, whom he gave the highest possible marks in every category. It was a first for the teacher, who rarely gave a perfect score. Yet the school rejected Timothée's application.

In an interview in *W Magazine*, Timothée states that the reason LaGuardia initially passed on him was his poor behavior record from middle school. In interviews, Timothée admits to misbehaving as a young teen. He has expressed gratitude toward those who had patience with him during this challenging time.

Shifman was stunned by the rejection. He felt so strongly that passing on this young actor would be a mistake that he barged into the principal's office during a private meeting to express his concern. Shifman urged the principal to reconsider Timothée's application, and she ended up taking his advice.

The decision was life-changing for Chalamet. Looking back, he describes the years he spent as a student and participant in the drama program at LaGuardia as having a huge impact on him. It was around this time that he realized how important acting was to him.

Once enrolled, Chalamet seemed to leave behind any behavior issues from his middle school years. He focused on his schoolwork and fully committed himself to acting, with the goal of pursuing a future in the arts.

Students who attended LaGuardia with Timothée say he had a knack for drawing audiences into his performances onstage. He played a number of different roles, each one allowing him to show a different side of himself as a performer. Some parts were dramatic. Others were comedic. This versatility made him stand out among the many talented students at the school.

PUTTING A SMILE ON HIS FACE

One of Timothée's early acting inspirations was the late Heath Ledger. Shortly after he began acting, Timothée attended a showing of *The Dark Knight* with his mother and maternal grandmother in Times Square. In this 2008 Batman film, Ledger played the iconic villain known as the Joker. Timothée was blown away by Ledger's Oscar-winning performance. It made Timothée realize that he wanted to bring characters to life the way Ledger had done with the Joker. Timothée describes Ledger as one of the actors who has shaped his artistry the most.

RAW TALENT AND KINDNESS

Timothée developed a strong identity at LaGuardia for both his acting ability and his personality. The school staged a regular talent show called Rising Stars in which Chalamet performed twice, rapping as an alter ego named Lil' Timmy Tim. Interviewers sometimes show him videos of these performances, which can still be found online. Although he now finds them embarrassing, he laughs goodheartedly at his younger self singing and dancing as the over-the-top character. He sees the videos as a reminder not to take himself too seriously.

Timothée was 15 when he got the idea for the character. At first he tried to recruit classmates to join him in the act. He recalls asking about 35 people before two friends, named Shiree and Desiree, agreed.[3] He had fun with the project, injecting it with plenty of comedic moments and fast dance moves.

“LaGuardia was . . . a fantastic place for me to go. It totally shaped who I am and who I was, and I just felt like I could be however I wanted to be.”[4]

—Timothée Chalamet, February 2025

Although some of his classmates saw him as the class clown, Timothée had many friends in high school, including some people with big ties to fame. While at LaGuardia, he dated classmate

Lourdes Leon, *left*, attended the Vanity Fair Oscar Party with Madonna in 2011, when Lourdes was a student at LaGuardia.

Lourdes Leon, the oldest daughter of pop music icon Madonna. Known as Lola to her friends, she has described Timothée as her first boyfriend. Timothée told talk show host Andy Cohen about a party he once attended at Lourdes's home, where they danced with her famous mother. He called it a really fun night.

Another fellow LaGuardia student was Ansel Elgort, an actor, singer, and DJ who went on to appear in *The Fault*

Timothée and former LaGuardia classmate Ansel Elgort attended a New York Knicks game in March 2018.

in Our Stars, *Baby Driver*, and other popular films. He and Timothée had the same drama teacher, were in the same science class, and played on LaGuardia's basketball team together. Years later, the two are still friends. When MTV asked both of them who was more popular in high school, they each insisted it was the other.

Timothée's teachers and classmates describe him as an especially kind person. High school can be a challenging time for students who struggle with feeling accepted.

Janelle Morillo was one of Timothée's classmates. In 2025, she posted a photo of herself with Timothée on TikTok. With it she wrote, "High school was not an easy or graceful time for me at certain points, and Timothée Chalamet was one of the people who was incredibly kind to me, and for that I am super grateful."[5]

RACKING UP ACTING CREDITS

In 2009, the year he started high school, Timothée got a small part in a TV movie called *Loving Leah*. He played a younger version of the movie's leading male character, Jake, in flashback scenes. His appearance on-screen was brief, but it gave him another television acting credit.

In 2011, Timothée appeared in his first off-Broadway show, *The Talls*. Broadway is the New York City district that is home to many big-production theaters. Off-Broadway shows are smaller and less commercial.

HIDDEN TALENT

When Timothée was in school, he tried his hand at graphic art. He made some extra cash by modifying Xbox 360 video game controllers and selling them. Many gamers enjoy using customized controllers in bright colors or with special graphics added. Timothée disassembled the controllers and painted fun designs on them before putting them back together. He made $30 selling three of the customized devices for ten dollars each.[6]

The Talls is a coming-of-age comedy set in the 1970s. Timothée played the main character's awkward younger brother, Nicholas.

The role was a small one, so the reviews for his performance were brief. A *New York Times* reviewer said that Timothée played the part "efficiently."[7] But being mentioned in the prestigious newspaper at all was a big accomplishment for such a young actor.

Timothée also acted in high school musical productions at LaGuardia. At first, however, he found it difficult to snag leading roles. This was because he looked younger than he was, and many of the roles were for older characters.

The school often chose students who looked older for these parts. This left Timothée to play less-significant characters. He auditioned for the musicals *Guys and Dolls* and *Hairspray*. But not even Shifman—one of Timothée's biggest advocates—would cast him in the leading roles.

In 2012, Timothée got the part of Oscar Lindquist in his high school's production of *Sweet Charity*. The play is about a dance hall hostess who dreams of finding true love. This was a bigger role for Timothée, and it gave him time to develop his skills and work toward other opportunities onstage.

Starring in a Broadway show is a dream for many up-and-coming actors, but the intimacy of off-Broadway shows has appeal as well.

According to Shifman, who directed *Sweet Charity*, one particular scene stood out. Timothée's character, who is afraid of small spaces, is trapped in an elevator with Charity. Shifman said, "I have to tell you something: in my entire life, I have never seen a more brilliant comic performance [than] Timmy gave in that scene."[8]

As a senior, Timothée won the role of the emcee in *Cabaret*. It was a commanding part, as this character guides the audience through the show. The emcee also sings some of the musical's most famous songs, including the opening number, "Willkommen," and "Money."

While LaGuardia offered a competitive environment in which to grow as an actor, Timothée hadn't built up enough experience to go after leading professional roles yet. He was making progress, however. Instead of winning

The spy thriller *Homeland*, starring Claire Daines and Damian Lewis, debuted in 2011 and ran for eight seasons on Showtime.

small, one-time roles on television, he landed a recurring role on a TV show. The USA Network series *Royal Pains* was about a doctor who starts a private medical practice for rich patients. Timothée played Luke, the nephew of one of the show's regular characters, for several episodes.

In 2012, he landed a recurring role on another TV show, the Showtime series *Homeland*. This role provided him with an opportunity to convey more of his acting ability. He played Finn Walden, the privileged son of the US vice president, in eight episodes of the show's second season. Although Finn had likable moments, he was extremely arrogant and angry. A critic from *Vulture* wrote that Timothée's age helped strengthen his performance of the immature character, but she also noted that Timothée gave Finn layers.

Timothée has criticized his performance in the role after watching himself in the show. He thinks he focused too much on the character as an antagonist instead of showing his human qualities as well. Critics, however, thought Timothée's performance revealed his character's loneliness and desperate need to be loved. They thought he portrayed Finn as a neglected boy whose selfishness was driven by a desire to be seen and understood.

INTO THE DEEP END

***Homeland*'s Finn Walden was Timothée's first major role on television. Although he wasn't new to acting when he was cast in the part, he still had a lot to learn. He compared the work to being thrown into the deep end of a pool but also says he loved the experience. Playing Finn helped Timothée build the confidence he needed as a performer to pursue bigger projects.**

When he graduated from LaGuardia High School in 2013, Timothée received the school's drama award. It appeared that more people than just Shifman realized that Timothée was a talented actor. A classmate at the graduation ceremony referred to Timothée's *Homeland* character in her commencement speech. She said that each and every member of their graduating class had a story to tell. And Timothée had already begun to tell his.

CHAPTER FOUR

PROGRESS AND CHALLENGES

Chalamet's parts on television led to small roles in films. In 2014, he appeared in two movies. Working on the film *Men, Women & Children* taught Chalamet that small roles can become even smaller after the editing process. He played Danny Vance, a teammate of the high school football star. By the time the movie was released, Chalamet's character appeared on-screen only a few brief times.

But critics took notice. Some were especially impressed by his ability to deliver a memorable performance in such a small role. Chalamet was disappointed, but he supported the film and his fellow

Timothée Chalamet attended the screening of the film *Men, Women & Children* in Toronto, Ontario, Canada, on September 6, 2014. >>

tiff.
Bell
VISA
L'ORÉAL
TELEFILM
Ontario

Chalamet and Sandler, *back right*, met to play basketball at a park in Soho, New York City, in 2023.

cast members by attending the movie's premiere and afterparty. One of those cast members was Adam Sandler.

When Chalamet was feeling discouraged about his shrunken part, Sandler was especially supportive of the younger actor. Despite their age difference, the two actors developed a lasting friendship. They share a love of basketball and still play in pickup games together when their busy schedules allow it.

Chalamet's second role that year came with *Interstellar*, a movie set in a bleak future where food shortages and dust storms threaten life on Earth. Matthew McConaughey plays Joseph Cooper, an ex-NASA pilot who returns to space to help find a new planet for humans.

Chalamet won the part of Tom, Joseph's son. The acclaimed Christoper Nolan directed the film. Although Tom was another small role, it was a pivotal one in the film.

When he saw *Interstellar,* Chalamet was especially surprised by one scene. During an important moment in the film, Joseph is in space watching video messages from Tom about his ongoing life on Earth. Chalamet had assumed the scene would show his acting skills, but only the audio played while the camera focused on Joseph's face, capturing his emotional reaction to Tom's updates. Chalamet understood why this was the better way to present the material, but he was disappointed that the audience could not see all he had put into the role.

Chalamet said, "I saw it, and I loved it, but I went home to my dad and wept for an hour because I had just figured

STARSTRUCK

Chalamet bonded with Matthew McConaughey during the production of *Interstellar.* McConaughey has said he saw natural talent in the young actor. Yet after they finished filming *Interstellar,* Chalamet was shocked to get a voicemail from McConaughey. The message made such an impression on Chalamet that he memorized every word. He later performed the voicemail as an impression of McConaughey during an interview. He said, "Timothée Chalamet. Yes, it's your movie dad, Cooper. It's your buddy, McConaughey, how are you, man? I'm just checking to see how that school's going, dorm move-in went . . . anyway, give a shout, let me know, give me a call, alright, bye."[1]

my part was bigger. They didn't even cut anything, I just figured—I don't know what I figured."[2] Once he dealt with his disappointment, he was able to inject his sense of humor into the situation.

He truly loved the film. When he shared in an interview that he'd seen it 12 times, an interviewer asked Chalamet if anyone noticed him in the movie theater. He joked, "Nobody noticed I was in the movie."[3]

Chalamet has said he felt a little like a fraud while promoting the film. He didn't feel worthy of being alongside famous actors such as Matthew McConaughey, Jessica Chastain, Anne Hathaway, and John Lithgow. But an article in *Esquire* said that Chalamet held his own among the film's great cast.

Interstellar became a big success at the box office. This made more people aware of Chalamet as an actor. He was still far from the household name he would become, but he was inching closer to getting that screen time he wanted so badly.

A QUICK STUDY

Between acting projects, Chalamet began attending Columbia University in 2014. It seemed like the next logical move for a young man who had just finished

Chalamet attended the premiere of *Interstellar* in Hollywood, California, in October 2014.

high school and came from a family that deeply valued traditional education. But after a year of juggling the demands of Columbia's courses with auditions and film shooting schedules, it felt like too much for Chalamet. He decided to drop out of the school where his grandfather had taught screenwriting classes.

He transferred to New York University's Gallatin School of Individualized Study. He hoped the more flexible schedule and coursework the school offered would help him balance his education with his acting pursuits. But in the end, he chose to drop out of this school as well to dedicate all his time to his acting career.

At first his mother didn't agree with this decision. She said, "I always encouraged him to pursue his passion and his dreams. However, I did not want him to leave Columbia. I had gone to Yale, and I just felt college would help him be a well-rounded individual."[4] *Interstellar* wasn't even out when Chalamet decided to leave college and focus on acting. She later said that although it was difficult for her to see then, he had made the right choice for himself.

A MAJOR UNDERTAKING

Chalamet majored in cultural anthropology during his time at Columbia University. This field involves the study of human societies and cultures. As an actor, he had focused most of his time on individual character studies. He described cultural anthropology as the total opposite. He found it humbling to learn about the ways people are products of their culture.

MORE REJECTION

Chalamet continued to audition for roles in films such as *The Maze Runner* and *Divergent*. Despite his acting ability, he was repeatedly passed over for these and many other mainstream projects. He once spent a week preparing a video audition only to receive no response after submitting it. Sitting around waiting for calls about parts was stressful for Chalamet.

He began receiving feedback that his thin build didn't fit the image many casting directors had for a leading man. His agent encouraged him to put on weight to increase his chances of getting roles in popular projects. Chalamet tried to gain weight but couldn't.

He realized he would not get every part he auditioned for. He once said that when it comes to acting, the answer is "no" more often than it is "yes." Because of this, Chalamet knew that learning to deal with rejection was an important step in becoming a successful actor. It is common for even the most talented actors to try out for parts and not get them.

Chalamet learned that rejection isn't personal and that he needed to develop a thick skin when it came to auditions. Ultimately, he built a new way of thinking about the roles he chose to audition for. Instead of seeing himself as wrong for a part, Chalamet began searching for roles that better suited him. This strategy led him to projects in which he could flourish as an actor.

LESSONS AND OPPORTUNITIES

Chalamet made the quality of his performances his top priority. He put forth his best effort in every step of the process, beginning with the audition. Chalamet values his sensitivity, knowing it makes him a better actor. It helps him communicate important emotions in the characters he portrays.

Chalamet read the part of Huey Falls in *The Tiny Problems of White People* at Manhattan's Jewish Community Center in December 2014. Chalamet's mother's family is Jewish.

As part of this preparation, Chalamet worked to understand what the actors playing opposite him needed. Sometimes this meant offering encouragement, while other times it meant not saying anything at all. He believed one of the responsibilities that comes with playing a leading role is helping to set the tone for the project. He made it his goal to be a supportive ensemble member. Chalamet believed that by leading with this attitude, everyone involved would work to help make one another and the project itself better.

The 2016 film *Miss Stevens* offered Chalamet the perfect opportunity to utilize all he had been learning. Although the movie had a low budget, the story appealed to him. And because *Miss Stevens* was independently produced, landing a part wasn't as tough as competing for a role in a movie from a big production company. These smaller projects, often called indie films, have developed a strong following among moviegoers. Some of the most well-known actors in the business got their big breaks in indie productions.

Chalamet played the part of Billy in *Miss Stevens*. The movie tells the story of a high school English teacher who chaperones three of her students on a trip to a state drama competition. Billy is one of the three young actors, and he impresses everyone around him when he takes the stage. Chalamet used his entire body for the role. He slouched, stuffed his hands into his pockets, and embodied a general awkwardness to help show how unsure of himself Billy was when he wasn't onstage.

Critics praised Chalamet's performance. At the competition, Billy delivers a monologue from the play *Death of a Salesman*. The *New York Times* called this scene a high point of the film,

At times, Chalamet has been compared to 1950s film star James Dean, who was known for his moody, intense roles in movies such as *Rebel Without a Cause*.

comparing Chalamet's stage presence to that of 1950s Hollywood star James Dean. The film won an award at the South by Southwest Film Festival, but the movie made next to nothing at the box office. Chalamet kept searching for his breakout role, the one that might catapult him to stardom.

COMING OF AGE

With his youthful appearance, Chalamet was frequently offered roles in coming-of-age films. He had shown through roles such as Finn Walden in *Homeland* that he was good at playing angst-ridden young men who make poor choices. In early 2016, Chalamet won the leading role of Jim Quinn in *Prodigal Son*.

In this off-Broadway play, Chalamet played a multilayered 17-year-old who is highly intelligent yet self-destructive, confident yet insecure. Critics thought the material suited him. The *New York Times* praised Chalamet's performance, for which he later won the

PLAYING A GIANT

In 2014, Chalamet told *Teen Vogue* that if he could play anyone from history, he would choose the late James Dean. Although Dean had starring roles in only three films, he is among the most iconic actors from the 1950s. His characters, like Chalamet's, were rebellious and emotional. Dean's life and career were cut short in 1955 when he died in a car accident at the age of 24.[5]

Chalamet, *back right*, appeared with the cast of *Hot Summer Nights* at the South by Southwest Festival in Austin, Texas, in 2017.

Lucille Lortel Award. This prize is given for outstanding achievement in off-Broadway theater.

John Patrick Shanley, who directed *Prodigal Son*, said musician Paul Simon noticed Chalamet's talent. Simon, who is known for being conservative with praise, was working on music for the play. He saw Chalamet perform during a dress rehearsal. "Kid's good," Simon told Shanley. After watching a bit longer, Simon added, "Kid's *very* good."[6]

Chalamet also played Daniel, the angst-ridden lead character in the film *Hot Summer Nights*, which was released in 2018. Part of this storyline involves Daniel selling illicit drugs. The choice takes him down a dark path. By playing the part of Daniel, Chalamet proved he could handle a leading film role.

CHAPTER FIVE

THE YEAR THAT CHANGED HIS CAREER

When director Luca Guadagnino was preparing to film a new movie called *Call Me by Your Name* in 2016, he knew he wanted Timothée Chalamet to play the leading role. The two men had originally met to discuss the indie project, which was based on the novel by André Aciman, three years earlier. Chalamet thought the meeting went great.

He and Guadagnino talked for hours and seemed to hit it off, but Chalamet didn't hear back from Guadagnino again. Guadagnino desperately wanted to make the film, but as is often the case in the entertainment industry, it took time for the project to come together.

At the 2018 Film Independent Spirit Awards, Chalamet took home the award for Best Male Lead for his work in *Call Me by Your Name*. >>

OFFW

Chalamet wasn't the typical leading man, but that was exactly what the director liked about him. Guadagnino likes people who break away from what is expected. He likes telling stories from nonconforming perspectives. He hoped this movie would be different from the films that were dominating the box office at the time. Set in 1983, the story was about Elio, a 17-year-old boy who falls in love with a male graduate student staying at his family's vacation home in Italy for the summer.

> **"The feeling of gratitude I have at the moment has less to do with individual achievement and more with the appreciation for the artists past honored in this category and all of the nominees of this year."[1]**
>
> **—Timothée Chalamet on his Oscar nomination for *Call Me by Your Name***

Once Chalamet was cast as Elio, he fully embraced the role. He headed to Italy about six weeks before filming

TOUGH LESSONS

Although Chalamet already knew French and English when he was cast in *Call Me by Your Name*, Italian was a different story. He said, "Learning the Italian was tough. I tried to really come at it from a purist perspective, really learn the grammar, syntax, and conjugations. And I'm proud of the job I do with the Italian in the movie, but I would maybe just do it phonetically if I had to go back and do it again."[2]

Chalamet spent about a month in Italy's Lombardy region during the filming of *Call Me by Your Name*. Most of the movie was shot in the town of Crema.

was set to begin. His character spoke three languages—English, French, and Italian—in the film. The first two weren't an issue for Chalamet, but he didn't know how to speak Italian. He took daily lessons so he could be convincing as a fluent speaker in the movie.

Guadagnino had high expectations for the film and everyone involved in it. The director wanted every detail to be just right. When a scene felt off to Guadagnino, he insisted that whatever wasn't right be changed, whether it was a small movement of a character or a seemingly random object in the background. Chalamet worked hard to match the director's vision of Elio's character.

When *Call Me by Your Name* was finished, it premiered at the 2017 Sundance Film Festival, the largest annual film festival in the United States. Early responses to the movie and Chalamet's performance were overwhelmingly positive. *Vanity Fair* pointed out that while the role wasn't his first movie performance, it felt like his debut. It seemed as if this film might be the big break that Chalamet had been dreaming of for so long.

FROM PAYCHECK TO PAYCHECK

Many people assume that appearing in movies leads to instant wealth, but for many actors, it takes time to earn a steady income. Independent film roles do not come with the high salaries that many mainstream parts do. Even as Chalamet was enjoying his greatest fame yet, he was still far from financially independent. At 22 years old, the young Oscar nominee had neither an apartment nor a credit card. He was staying with friends between projects.

SOMETHING NEW

Roles in indie films were coming to Chalamet steadily now. Shortly after he finished filming *Call Me by Your Name*, he started working on a new project. It would be unlike anything he had done before. *Hostiles* is a nontraditional Western. It features Christian Bale, Rosamund Pike, Jesse Plemons, and many other actors whom director Scott Cooper wanted to be in the movie so badly that he created roles for them to play.

Chalamet was the only actor with a lead role who actually auditioned for the film. Chalamet's résumé was growing, but Cooper had never seen any of his work. *Call Me by Your Name* had not been released yet, so Cooper didn't yet know how capable an actor Chalamet was.

Chalamet had been fortunate to land the leading role in *Call Me by Your Name* without an audition. Most actors, especially newer ones, must go through this grueling process even after making names for themselves in the business. If they are lucky, they get called back for a second or even a third audition before the casting director and others feel certain they are making the best possible choice.

Some actors feel nervous before an audition, but for Chalamet, the hardest time is afterward. He says, "I'm a big hypocrite in that I believe that the most important part of any audition is the second you leave the room. If you can leave and not beat yourself up, it's going to help you next time."[3]

Although it wasn't the first time Chalamet had worked with famous actors, he could not help but feel starstruck on meeting Bale. Chalamet greatly admired Bale's work,

Chalamet said he learned a lot while working with Christian Bale on *Hostiles*, including how to set the tone for a film's cast.

especially his portrayal of Patrick Bateman in *American Psycho*. Chalamet said, "I remember him asking me to repeat my name so he could hear it better and commit it to memory. My voice got caught in my throat, not really being able to get it out, thinking: Why, for the first time in my 20 years on this planet, is my mouth not following what my brain wants it to?"[4] After finding his composure, Chalamet managed to ask the Oscar winner numerous questions about acting, and Bale was kind enough to chat with him about their shared craft.

In *Hostiles*, Chalamet played Private Philippe DeJardin, a US soldier who is part of the movie's dangerous mission of escorting a Cheyenne war chief and his family from New Mexico to their ancestral homeland in Montana. DeJardin is not the leading role, but he is a standout character in the film. With no combat experience and a distaste for violence, DeJardin was another character Chalamet could bring to life with his natural sensitivity.

Critics praised Chalamet's performance, saying he held his own in scenes with Bale, who was a much more accomplished actor. Despite its praise from critics, *Hostiles* was a huge disappointment at the box office. The movie, which cost $39 million to make, brought in less than $36 million worldwide.[5]

MAKING CONNECTIONS

Making a film often takes months. During this time, the actors may form strong bonds with their fellow actors, directors, and other people involved with the project. Chalamet formed this type of friendship with director Greta Gerwig while they were filming *Lady Bird*. Following the project, Gerwig said that she and Chalamet are so at ease with each other that they can talk for more than an hour over the phone without realizing how much time has passed.

AWARD-NOMINATED PROJECTS

Chalamet's next indie project was *Lady Bird*, a film written and directed by Greta Gerwig and starring Saoirse Ronan. In the future, Gerwig would experience great success with her blockbuster movie *Barbie*, but in 2016, she was still largely unknown. Although Gerwig had written screenplays and acted, *Lady Bird* was her directorial debut.

Chalamet first met Saoirse Ronan on the set of *Lady Bird* in 2017, and they have remained close friends ever since.

She discovered Chalamet when he was performing in *Prodigal Son*. Gerwig likes finding actors onstage, as she feels the theater setting gives them the space to really show what they can do. Gerwig left the theater impressed with what she had seen of Chalamet and ended up casting him as Kyle Scheible, a teen antagonist, in *Lady Bird*.

The film is named for its main character, Christine "Lady Bird" McPherson, an independent teenager who is exploring who she is and who she wants to be. Kyle, a moody musician, is one of her love interests in the film. One of the things Chalamet liked best about the movie was that it offered a fresh take on a female coming-of-age story. Unlike many films about young women on the verge of adulthood, *Lady Bird* was not defined by the main character's romantic relationships.

Not wanting to repeat the mistake he felt he had made with Finn in *Homeland*, Chalamet decided to approach Kyle differently. In addition to the character's less desirable traits, Chalamet wanted to show Kyle's humanity. To Chalamet, a good performance requires portraying all sides of a character. In the case of Kyle, this meant showing his emotions and suffering. Chalamet said Gerwig's great writing made that easy.

The film was a hit at the box office, bringing in more than $79 million. This was a considerable amount, especially compared with the movie's modest $10 million budget.[6] *Lady Bird* was nominated for four Golden Globes. The film won for Best Motion Picture—Musical or Comedy, and Ronan won the award for Best Actress in a Motion Picture. The film also earned five Oscar nominations, including Best Actress, Best Director, and Best Picture.

Chalamet did not receive any nominations for his role in *Lady Bird*, but his performance in *Call Me by Your Name* earlier that year earned him a Golden Globe nomination for Best Actor in a Motion Picture—Drama and a nomination for an Oscar for Best Actor. He was shocked to hear his name the morning the 2018 Academy Award nominations were announced. Critics and fans had been talking about his performance in *Call Me by Your*

Name since its release. Many people thought Chalamet deserved awards for his role of Elio, but just receiving the nominations was an incredible honor. Although Chalamet did not win either award, the nominations sent a clear message that he had joined the ranks of the best actors in contemporary film.

TAKING A STAND AGAINST SEXUAL ASSAULT

In early 2018, Chalamet made a bold decision. A few months earlier, he had filmed a movie called *A Rainy Day in New York* with director Woody Allen. The film's cast included Elle Fanning, Rebecca Hall, Selena Gomez, and Griffin Newman. Just weeks after filming ended, an editorial penned by Dylan Farrow, the director's adopted daughter, appeared in the *Los Angeles Times*.

In it, she questioned why actors continued to work with Woody Allen. Farrow had accused Allen of sexually assaulting her in 1992, when she was seven years old. After an investigation into the matter, no charges were filed, but decades later, Farrow stood by her claims.

The piece became part of a broader discussion about sexual assault called the #MeToo Movement. Sexual assault survivors use the hashtag when sharing their

Chalamet and Selena Gomez filmed on location in New York City for *A Rainy Day in New York* in September 2017.

stories online. Many women revealed that they had been abused by powerful men in film production and other industries.

Chalamet announced on Instagram that he was donating his salary from the movie to charity to show his support for survivors of sexual assault. Hall and Newman also decided to donate their earnings to charity. Although Chalamet's contracts prevented him from speaking about his decision to work with Allen, Chalamet stated that he did not want to profit from his work on the film.

CHAPTER SIX

SHOWING HIS RANGE

Chalamet wasted no time getting back to work after the whirlwind of his Academy Award nomination for *Call Me by Your Name*. Although he would always be linked to that film, of which he was incredibly proud, it was time to move on. The Oscar nomination led to a series of TV appearances and other interviews, so he'd been spending a lot more time talking about his work than actually working. A Netflix film called *The King* provided Chalamet the opportunity to focus on his acting again. Filming began in June 2018.

The movie is a retelling of Shakespeare's play *Henry V* with updated dialogue, starring Chalamet as

Playing the lead role in *The King* was a key stepping stone in Chalamet's early career. >>

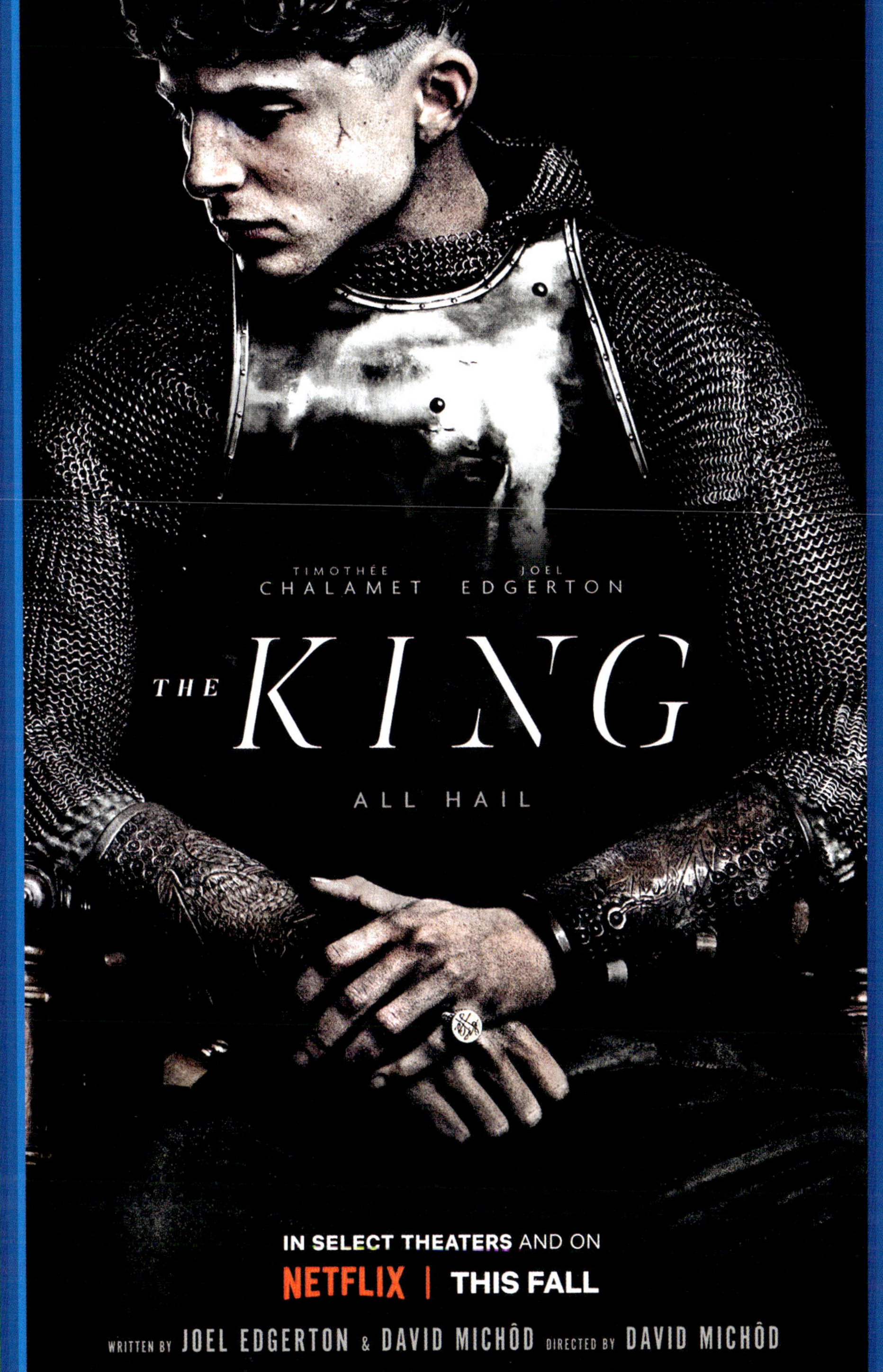
TIMOTHÉE
CHALAMET
JOEL
EDGERTON
THE KING
ALL HAIL
IN SELECT THEATERS AND ON
NETFLIX | THIS FALL
WRITTEN BY JOEL EDGERTON & DAVID MICHÔD DIRECTED BY DAVID MICHÔD

the British king opposite Robert Pattinson as the son of France's King Charles VI. Chalamet's role stood in stark contrast to his previous work, and both he and the overall project received positive reviews. His young appearance offered him an advantage, as the character is a boy who is thrust into a position he isn't prepared to take on. *Vanity Fair*'s review spoke about Chalamet slowly ascending to the role as the character gradually rose to his duty.

IN THE SPOTLIGHT

Chalamet had become royalty of sorts off camera as well. Working was a valuable distraction from all the new attention he was receiving. The success of *Call Me by Your Name* and *Lady Bird* had catapulted him into the pop culture spotlight. He was trying to make sense of his sudden fame, continue to work, and not lose connections that helped ground him.

At times, he felt tense and confused. Spending time with friends made him feel as if nothing had really changed, but things had indeed changed. He was entering a new and very different part of his life.

While filming *The King*, Chalamet met Lily-Rose Depp, the daughter of actor Johnny Depp. She played Catherine of Valois, who married Henry V to solidify a political

Chalamet and Depp coordinated the outfits they wore to attend the Venice Film Festival in September 2019.

alliance between England and France. Off-screen, the two actors began dating, which Chalamet quickly learned was more challenging due to their fame.

The press was now watching Chalamet much more closely, eager to write about both his professional and his private life. He and Depp managed to keep their romance quiet for a while, but news of their relationship went public when the press spotted them kissing in New York later that year. The two chose not to talk about their private lives in interviews.

GOING ALL IN

In October 2018, a movie that Chalamet filmed with Steve Carell opened in theaters. *Beautiful Boy* is a powerful

Director Felix van Groeningen, Timothée Chalamet, and Steve Carell, *left to right*, discussed the making of *Beautiful Boy* at Build Studio in New York City in October 2018.

drama about a real-life father-son relationship that is based on the book *Beautiful Boy: A Father's Journey Through His Son's Addiction*. The role of the father, David Sheff, was a big departure for Carell, who was better known for his comedic roles. Chalamet played the son, Nic Sheff, who battled methamphetamine use. Chalamet had taken on dramatic parts in the past, but playing Nic was one of the more challenging roles of his career.

He auditioned for the part many times. Nearly every young actor in the business tried to win the role. Once he was cast, he began preparing for the part by talking to people in recovery from addiction, including Nic Sheff himself.

"There was nothing about Nic and meeting him that rubbed me of addiction, or whatever my stereotype would've been of that at the time," Chalamet explained. "And that was the learning grace of this movie for me. Addiction doesn't have a face, it has no preferred class, or gender, or race."[1]

Although Chalamet had been told to gain weight earlier in his career, this role required Chalamet to lose weight. To show the physical effects of substance use that Nic had experienced, Chalamet dropped 18 pounds (8.2 kg).[2] He did so under the supervision of medical professionals.

Movie scenes are often filmed out of order, so the plan was to shoot the scenes in which Nic weighed the

CLOSE BUT NO AWARDS

Chalamet was nominated for several awards for his role of Nic in *Beautiful Boy*. They included a Golden Globe, a British Academy of Film and Television Arts (BAFTA) Award, and a Screen Actors Guild Award—each for Best Supporting Actor. Reviewers praised his work. Kenneth Turan of the *Los Angeles Times* said, "With moments reminiscent of James Dean . . . Chalamet both echoes the best of what's come before and makes the part his own, allowing us to feel we've never seen a character like this. If you want to witness what honesty, authenticity and a remarkable gift can accomplish, this is the place to go."[3] Despite many positive reviews for his work in the movie, he did not take home any major awards.

least amount first. That way, Chalamet could regain weight over a short break and return to filming looking healthier for the remainder of the movie's scenes. He soon learned that it wasn't going to be quite that easy. After depriving himself of food for so long, his body had to be reintroduced to food gradually. He eventually gained the weight back, but it took longer than he had expected.

At times, it was tough to get the role just right. Chalamet was dedicated to making every part of the film exactly as director Felix van Groeningen envisioned it. Chalamet shot one particularly challenging scene, which took place in a diner, 20 times before everyone was pleased with the result.[4]

Chalamet's portrayal of Nic led to his second Golden Globe nomination, this time for Best Supporting Actor. Although he didn't win the award, he was grateful that so many people saw the film. He hoped it would raise awareness of the substance use that affects so many people worldwide.

LITTLE WOMEN

Chalamet reunited with Gerwig when she directed a new film version of the classic book *Little Women*. When she asked him to play Theodore "Laurie" Laurence in the film,

Chalamet hadn't yet read the popular novel. Once he did, he thought Laurie was a great character, but he also admitted that he would take any role Gerwig wanted him to play.

Laurie was a longtime friend of the four March sisters. He was closest with Jo. The project also allowed Chalamet to reunite with Saoirse Ronan, who played Jo. In interviews he had called Ronan one of his favorite people to work with.

CHALAMET'S STYLING OF LAURIE

Jacqueline Durran, the costume designer for *Little Women*, saw that Timothée Chalamet had a keen eye for fashion. She decided to involve him in styling his character for the film. Instead of telling Chalamet what to wear, she hung multiple costumes in his trailer, encouraging him to select and pair items that he imagined Laurie might choose himself. Chalamet's strong sense of style, combined with his understanding of the character, helped him dress for the part.

Critics praised Chalamet's portrayal of Laurie. A *Vox* review even insisted that it would be difficult to imagine anyone else in the part. The movie did well at the box office, making more than $100 million worldwide.[5] Still, it was largely overlooked at award ceremonies. Some fans wondered if this was because the movie was stereotypically seen as being for girls. Even Chalamet himself was somewhat influenced by this view, but he was quickly called out by another important woman in his life, his sister.

Chalamet and Ronan, who appeared together for the second time in *Little Women*, are known for having great chemistry on set.

He relayed the conversation to Jimmy Fallon during an appearance on *The Tonight Show* in 2019 before the film's release. Chalamet explained, "I was saying it to my sister yesterday. I was like, 'Man, if I have daughters one day, I want them to see it.' And she was like, 'If you have sons,' and it's true."[6]

MOMENTS OF PRIVATE TIME

Chalamet was working so much that he always seemed to have at least one project in the works and another coming out soon. When *The King* was ready for its 2019 release, he and Lily-Rose Depp attended its premiere at the Venice Film Festival together. The couple were still dating, but the press often made spending time together difficult. Whenever Chalamet and Depp were in public spaces, photographers always seemed to be lurking nearby.

Following *The King*'s premiere, Chalamet and Depp spent an afternoon on a yacht in Capri, Italy. He recalls, "I went to bed that night thinking that was one of the best days of my life. I was on this boat all day with someone I really loved, and closing my eyes, I was like, indisputably, 'That was great.' And then waking up to all these [paparazzi] pictures, and feeling embarrassed, and looking. . . . All pale?"[7]

FRENCH CONNECTIONS

Playing Henry V in *The King* gave Chalamet a chance to use his fluency in French briefly on-screen. He put his language skills to use in two of the movie's scenes. In the first one, Henry V speaks with a French messenger sent to him by Pattinson's character. In the other scene, Chalamet plays opposite Depp's character, who speaks only French. The 2021 film *The French Dispatch* offered no such opportunity, despite its setting and title, because Chalamet's character was an American.

The images had already gone viral, eliciting many hateful comments online. Some people made hurtful comments about Chalamet's appearance. Memes making fun of the actor began circulating. A few months after their visit to Italy, they ended their relationship.

WORKING TOGETHER, SUDDENLY APART

Shortly after he finished filming *Little Women*, Chalamet started working on a new film called *The French Dispatch*.

In *The French Dispatch*, Chalamet's character, Zefferelli, has a brief romantic relationship with Frances McDormand's character, journalist Lucinda Krementz, *center*.

This comedy from director Wes Anderson told three stories from *The French Dispatch*, a fictional magazine. Chalamet played Zefferelli, a young revolutionary who becomes the face of a student protest movement featured in one of the stories.

The movie's cast included many experienced and talented actors. Chalamet was especially grateful for the chance to work with Frances McDormand and Bill Murray. He learned a lot from them while on the job and enjoyed their company at the end of the day. He later said that Murray often cracked jokes at the dinner table.

The cast stayed in the same hotel in Angouleme, France, so they were able to spend a lot of time together off the movie set.

The movie's release date was delayed by the COVID-19 pandemic. Acting projects that Chalamet had lined up were put on hold or canceled. In early 2020, he had spent three weeks in London rehearsing for a play called *4,000 Miles*, only to have the production shut down a couple of weeks before performances were to begin. Movie theaters, restaurants, and most nonessential businesses closed to help prevent the virus from spreading. People all over the world began isolating themselves as quarantines began.

The pandemic continued as scientists developed vaccines for the virus. Eventually, people returned to working and socializing in person, but life didn't feel the same for many people. Reflecting later, Chalamet said he thought the period helped him grow up.

CHAPTER SEVEN

FROM INDIE FILMS TO BLOCKBUSTERS

One of Chalamet's projects that was stalled by the pandemic was a film adaptation of the classic science fiction novel *Dune*. The part of Paul Atreides was another role that many young actors wanted to play, but director Denis Villeneuve always had Chalamet in mind for the leading part. They filmed it before the 2020 shutdowns that brought much of the film industry to a halt, but the pandemic made releasing the movie a challenge.

Although fans of the original book expressed excitement for the film, many people were hesitant to spend time in theaters with the virus still spreading. The movie finally premiered in September 2021 at

***Dune: Part One* was Chalamet's biggest movie to date.** >>

TIMOTHÉE CHALAMET
REBECCA FERGUSON
OSCAR ISAAC
JOSH BROLIN
STELLAN SKARSGÅRD
DAVE BAUTISTA
STEPHEN McKINLEY HENDERSON
ZENDAYA
CHANG CHEN
SHARON DUNCAN-BREWSTER
WITH CHARLOTTE RAMPLING
WITH JASON MOMOA
AND JAVIER BARDEM
IT BEGINS
DUNE
SEE IT IN THEATERS
AND ON HBOmax
OCTOBER 22
WARNER BROS. PICTURES AND LEGENDARY PICTURES PRESENT A LEGENDARY PICTURES PRODUCTION
PG-13
LEGENDARY
Dolby Cinema REAL D 3D FILMED FOR IMAX
WARNER BROS.

Chalamet and Rebecca Ferguson, who played his mother in both *Dune* movies, had very different acting techniques. Chalamet was more serious, and Ferguson was more lighthearted.

the Venice Film Festival. It was later released to theaters around the world and made available for streaming on HBO Max for a limited time beginning late that October. Streaming just-released films became common during the pandemic to allow new movies to reach audiences.

Chalamet wanted to be part of the new adaptation from the beginning. He especially wanted to work with Villeneuve, who had directed other successful sci-fi films such as *Arrival* and *Blade Runner 2049*. What Chalamet liked most about the director's previous work was that even amid big sci-fi ideas and impressive visual effects, the characters were always at the center of his stories. Chalamet thought audiences would relate to Paul's struggles, which included finding his identity. As someone who had struggled with this himself, he was confident he could do the character justice.

A SECOND SISTER

Chalamet and his *Dune* costar Zendaya became great friends while filming the first movie. Although the two actors had little on-screen time together in that installment, they were able to spend time together when the cameras weren't rolling. In interviews, Chalamet said Zendaya has become like a sister to him. He appreciates her energy and considers her a breath of fresh air. The two also bonded over stories about how much they enjoyed working with director Luca Guadagnino.

Taking on the role meant committing to a second film, as the remake split the complex novel into two parts, but this didn't deter Chalamet from the project. As long as *Dune: Part One* did well at the box office, he was virtually guaranteed the leading role in the sequel. After acting primarily in indie films for several years, Chalamet was now the star of a movie from a major studio. Warner Bros. Pictures produced the film, which had a $165 million budget, in partnership with Legendary Entertainment.[1] For Chalamet, appearing in the leading role would pave the way for parts in other big-budget projects.

Chalamet relished the chance to work with the other actors involved in the film, such as Josh Brolin, Jason

Momoa, and Zendaya, but he also found the opportunity intimidating. When he got the part in the film, Chalamet said he suffered from imposter syndrome. This is the fear that others will soon discover one's true lack of ability.

He'd never been cast in a project of this scope before. Although he had traveled to Europe to film movies such as *Call Me by Your Name* and *The French Dispatch*, appearing in *Dune: Part One* would mean filming in multiple foreign locations, including the United Arab Emirates, Hungary, Jordan, and Norway.

Once filming began, Chalamet felt a huge responsibility to move within the framework of director Denis Villeneuve's vision for the film. Chalamet compared it to not disrupting a wheel while it's turning. He knew that Villeneuve had cherished the *Dune* books as a young person. The director said in an interview that what he was most afraid of in making the film was disappointing his own teenage self. Chalamet also did not want to disappoint Villeneuve or the many other fans of the series.

Dune: Part One was a big success, grossing more than $400 million and making the production of a sequel likely.[2] Chalamet was pleased with the film, but as he waited for the next phase of the project, he was also preparing to work on a completely different movie.

Chalamet stated that the amount of singing and dancing made his role in *Wonka* his most challenging to that point.

This one was less dark and more uplifting, which is exactly what many of his fans were looking forward to.

PURE IMAGINATION

Many years before Chalamet was born, actor Gene Wilder starred in the musical film *Willy Wonka & the Chocolate Factory*. The movie was based on the 1964 book *Charlie and the Chocolate Factory* by Roald Dahl, telling the story of a young boy named Charlie who finds a highly coveted golden ticket within the wrapper of a candy bar. The voucher leads Charlie to an adventurous tour of a magical candy-making facility owned by the title character. Johnny Depp played the role of Willy Wonka in the 2005 remake that used the book's title. Both movies were popular with children and even many adults.

In late 2021, director Paul King began filming a prequel to the original movie. It was called simply *Wonka*. Unlike the previous movies, it focused on Willy Wonka as a young person, and King chose Chalamet to play the character who dreamed of having his own chocolate shop. The new project was a companion piece to the original movie starring Wilder.

Chalamet hadn't performed in a musical since he was in high school, but he was excited for the challenge. The leading role in *Wonka* was physically demanding, requiring him to sing, dance, and bring the same enthusiasm and perfection to numerous takes. He worked with a vocal coach to perform six original songs for the film. He also sang a new version of "Pure Imagination," which Wilder had performed in the first movie.

Many fans who had been introduced to Chalamet in *Dune: Part One* wondered if the young

LIKE A KID IN A CANDY STORE

Chalamet and his *Wonka* character share a love of chocolate. The actor's favorite candies are Junior Mints, Milk Duds, and Raisinets. He says he likes to pop about a dozen Milk Duds in his mouth at once. First, he sucks all the chocolate off, and then he soaks in the caramel flavor. Chalamet's other favorite movie snacks are watermelon Sour Patch Kids and popcorn with extra butter. He admits he doesn't always feel so great the next day.

actor did his own singing in *Wonka*. The two roles showcased completely different skill sets. Critics confirmed that Chalamet was indeed the singer, praising his vocal abilities. Director Paul King even compared him to Bing Crosby, the actor known for the beloved musical *White Christmas*.

> **"Singing 'Pure Imagination,' that almost felt sacrilegious to go near, 'cause Gene Wilder does it so perfectly. . . . But my version of the song is sort of the send-off in our movie. The song is the same, but the messaging is a little different."**[4]
>
> —Timothée Chalamet on performing "Pure Imagination" in *Wonka*

Reviews of the movie itself were less generous. The *New York Times* said *Wonka* was too eager to please and lasted too long, but audiences still went to see it. The movie, which cost $120 million to make, raked in more than $634 million worldwide.[3] Chalamet had now shown he could be a successful leading actor in a range of projects.

REUNITING WITH GUADAGNINO

Chalamet's second film project with Luca Guadagnino came along in 2021. Since the filming of *Call Me by Your Name*, both men had wanted to work with each other again. They had forged a friendship through that first project. When Chalamet learned of his Oscar nomination for the movie, he traveled all the way to Italy to celebrate the milestone with Guadagnino. Finally their schedules had aligned and the right project had come along to reunite them professionally once more.

The new movie was very different from *Call Me by Your Name*. The premise of *Bones and All* made it sound like a dark comedy. The story followed two teenage cannibals on a road trip across the United States in the 1980s.

The book on which the movie was based, however, was a teen romance. The relationship between Chalamet's character, Lee, and Taylor Russell's character, Maren, is central to the plot. Until Lee meets Maren, he lives a lonely life, largely due to his cannibalistic habits, but when he discovers that she shares his taste for human flesh, the pair find comfort in their shared secret.

As Guadagnino and Chalamet worked on the new film, the director noticed how much Chalamet had grown as an actor. He was much more confident than he had been six years earlier. Guadagnino saw that Chalamet wanted to take more risks on-screen. This was evident just in Chalamet's interest in portraying such an unusual character, but Guadagnino liked the fact that Chalamet was constantly pushing himself. At times, the director

Chalamet and *Bones and All* costar Taylor Russell immediately connected during filming, as both prioritize empathy and compassion in their acting.

even stepped back and, instead of providing detailed direction, allowed Chalamet and Russell to follow their instincts in certain scenes.

Guadagnino thought that persuading a major studio to finance a movie about teenage cannibals would likely have been an uphill battle, so he sought funding from numerous smaller production companies. This made *Bones and All* another indie project, with a budget of about $16 million. The upside of this low budget meant it wouldn't take long for the movie to make a profit if it did well at the box office, but the film made just $15 million worldwide.[5] With other major projects in the works, however, the box office failure of *Bones and All* was just a minor setback for Chalamet.

THE NEXT CHAPTER

Chalamet began filming *Dune: Part Two* in 2022. The success of the first installment set the bar high for the sequel. In addition to its commercial success, the first film won six Academy Awards, including Best Cinematography and Best Visual Effects. Although it didn't win the award for Best Picture, it was nominated for the honor.

Along with Chalamet, Zendaya returned for the sequel. New cast members included Austin Butler and Florence Pugh. Chalamet and Butler had some intense fighting scenes in the new movie. In an interview with *Men's Health*, Chalamet said Tom Cruise's performance in *Top Gun: Maverick* was a big inspiration for him. After meeting Chalamet in 2019, Cruise encouraged the younger actor to train as thoroughly as possible for his stunt work. Villeneuve noticed how prepared Chalamet was for these scenes.

Zendaya and Chalamet showed up for a *Dune: Part Two* press conference in matching jumpsuits.

The film was set to premiere on November 3, 2023, but strikes by the writing and acting unions, which began in the spring, changed the plan. Writers and actors in the United States were unhappy that their pay was not increased to match the new age of streaming shows and movies to mass audiences. Although *Dune: Part Two* had already been filmed, the strikes prevented the cast from promoting the movie.

It is common for a movie's actors to do interviews in the weeks and months ahead of a movie's release. These appearances, which create excitement for the film, can have a big impact on box office numbers. But during a strike, artists avoid working until the dispute has been resolved. That work includes promotional interviews.

By November, both strikes had ended, but Warner Bros. Pictures pushed the release date to March 1, 2024. This would give the cast time to raise excitement for the release. Despite the

HIS BIGGEST PAYCHECK

In 2023, Chalamet worked on the highest-paying project of his career to date. It wasn't a movie or a TV series, though. It was an ad for Bleu de Chanel, a men's fragrance by the popular French fashion house Chanel. It was his first time working with the renowned Martin Scorsese, who directed the satirical 90-second commercial. Chalamet was paid $35 million for the ad.[6]

long wait, *Dune: Part Two* enjoyed great success at the box office. The movie had an especially high budget of $190 million.[7] But the film made more than $714 million worldwide.[8] Chalamet was now among the stars who consistently drew audiences to projects from major production companies.

A NEW LOVE

By the fall of 2023, rumors of a new romantic relationship in Chalamet's life had been swirling for several months. They linked him to Kylie Jenner, a famous media personality known for her makeup company and her family's reality TV show, *Keeping Up with the Kardashians*. Neither Chalamet nor Jenner confirmed the rumors at first, but the press regularly reported when they were spotted together. After attending a Beyoncé concert and a tennis match at the US Open together in September 2023, the couple went more public with their relationship. By December, Jenner was openly referring to Chalamet as her boyfriend.

As someone who has worked hard to keep his private life private, Chalamet was sometimes criticized for dating such a public person. *GQ* reporter Daniel Riley even pointed out during an interview with the actor that he

Chalamet and Kylie Jenner attended the red carpet event for the David Di Donatello Awards at Cinecittà Studios in Rome, Italy, in May 2025.

was dating one of the four most-followed people on Instagram. But Chalamet does not give in to pressure to share more information about the relationship.

The couple spends time together and supports each other at important events. When Chalamet hosted *Saturday Night Live* in November 2023, Jenner attended the afterparty with him. When she was honored with an Innovator Award from *WSJ Magazine*, Chalamet attended the ceremony with her at New York City's Museum of Modern Art. One of their biggest outings yet came in January 2024. Chalamet brought Jenner as his date to the Golden Globes, where he was nominated for Best Actor in a Motion Picture—Musical or Comedy for his role in *Wonka*.

CHAPTER EIGHT

LIKE A ROLLING STONE

Chalamet has portrayed characters in a wide range of time periods. *Little Women*'s Laurie grew up in the late 1860s. *Prodigal Son*'s Jim Quinn was a teenager a century later. *Call Me by Your Name*'s Elio Perlman was on the brink of adulthood in the 1980s. And Paul Atreides lives more than 20,000 years in the future.

While he had to live up to the images that writers and directors had created for these characters, they were all fictional. This allowed Chalamet to make the characters somewhat his own. But as he learned when he portrayed Nic Sheff in *Beautiful Boy*, playing a real-life person is different.

Chalamet and costar Elle Fanning filmed a scene for *A Complete Unknown* in Hoboken, New Jersey, the state in which most of the movie was filmed. >>

For his next role as legendary folk singer Bob Dylan in the movie *A Complete Unknown*, Chalamet had to do some homework about the real-life character he was playing. He knew almost nothing about Dylan, who has always preferred privacy. Dylan, who ascended to stardom in the 1960s, never embraced mainstream popularity. He repeatedly turned down requests for interviews, and he rarely showed up at award shows even when he was nominated. In 2016, when he won the Nobel Prize for Literature, he didn't even attend the ceremony.

Still, his music became an unofficial soundtrack of an era. The 1960s was a time of tremendous political, social, and cultural upheaval. Dylan's songs reflected the way many young people were feeling about the Vietnam War (1954–1975), civil rights, and their own identities.

Although it was harder to make this character his own, Chalamet found some of himself in Dylan. Both men had experienced a rapid rise to fame in their early twenties. This mutual experience gave Chalamet some insight into the music icon. Dylan never agreed to meet with him, so he had to use other methods to gain more understanding of the man behind the music.

Chalamet watched many YouTube videos of Dylan performing his songs as a young man. One recording

Chalamet studied Dylan's mannerisms and the way he played the guitar and harmonica to fine-tune his character. Dylan is shown here in 1968 or 1969.

that made a particularly big impression on the actor was a rendition of "It Ain't Me, Babe," which Dylan performed with fellow musician Joan Baez. The two had a romantic relationship early in their careers, which was depicted in the movie.

Chalamet watched this video repeatedly. He said, "That was when I really slowed down [the video], cause it's fascinating the way Bob observes her, and how he refuses eye contact in that video."[1] He used the added insight he had gained for his portrayal of the singer.

Chalamet reached out to Austin Butler for advice on performing the songs in *A Complete Unknown*. Although they had played enemies in *Dune: Part Two*, the two actors became good friends in real life while filming that project. They often discuss creative topics with each other.

AN INSIDE LOOK

As part of his preparation to play Bob Dylan, Chalamet visited the singer's childhood homes in Minnesota. Dylan lived in both Duluth and Hibbing while growing up in the state. The current owner of the house in Hibbing shared drawings and notes that the singer left behind. Although many of Dylan's writings have been circulated on the internet over the years, these had not. Chalamet said they were helpful in learning about the singer's sense of the world and drive to become a musician.

Having portrayed legendary singer Elvis Presley in a 2022 biopic, Butler had been in a similar situation. He shared some of the things that had helped him when he played Presley.

BECOMING DYLAN

Chalamet took lessons to learn how to play both the guitar and the harmonica in *A Complete Unknown*. Although he had played guitar briefly for *Call Me by Your Name*, the character he portrayed in that movie wasn't a professional musician. Chalamet was also going to sing in the new film.

He had several scenes in which his character would perform live in front of audiences. To prepare, the production company had him record all the songs ahead of time. The plan was for the audio to play during those scenes, but Chalamet didn't think the recordings worked.

He sounded a lot like the singer, but the recordings came across as too polished, as if they had been recorded in a studio—because they had. Dylan's live music didn't

Chalamet knew only a few guitar chords before taking on the role of Dylan, so he took lessons from instructor Larry Saltzman for five years.

sound perfect, and Chalamet wanted his versions of the songs to sound authentic. He decided to perform the music live on set.

Rob Paparozzi, a harmonica coach who worked with Chalamet for the film, did an interview in *GQ*. In it, he admitted that he hadn't heard of Chalamet before working with him on the Dylan movie. Paparozzi's family knew who the actor was, though. His son told him that Chalamet had starred in the *Dune* movies. His grandkids told him that Chalamet was Willy Wonka. Paparozzi then watched the movies to get a better sense of the person he'd be teaching.

He told *GQ* that there is a difference between learning to play this instrument and copying the way another musician plays it. He said that the latter is an extremely difficult task, perhaps even harder to accomplish when one is trying to imitate Dylan. As with the way he sings, the musician has his own quirky way of playing the harmonica. But Paparozzi thought Chalamet's performances were spot-on.

Playing such a reclusive person came with its challenges, but Chalamet was determined to capture this important part of the character. He did this by isolating himself from family and friends while he filmed the project. For three months, he took a break from his real life. He didn't use his cell phone, and he didn't allow his loved ones to visit the set. He didn't want to be distracted from his performance even for a moment.

With every little detail he added to the character, Chalamet was becoming more and more like Dylan.

GIVING THANKS

Leading up to the release of *A Complete Unknown*, Chalamet did many interviews. Several journalists asked him what he might say to Dylan if he ever met him. Chalamet told the Associated Press that he would thank the singer for the music he has given the world.

He already resembled the musician, and he was now behaving and sounding like him as well. But to match Dylan's full appearance, Chalamet needed to put on some weight. In the past he had resisted gaining weight to please movie producers, but this situation felt different to him. He decided to gain 20 pounds (9 kg) for the role.[2]

FIRST IMPRESSIONS

When news about the biopic began spreading, many people had opinions about the project. Some Dylan fans worried that the movie wouldn't be able to capture the true essence of the singer. Others wondered whether Chalamet was the right actor for the role. Some people told him not to take the role because they suspected it would be a near-impossible one to pull off.

Bob Dylan himself responded to news of the movie by posting a statement on the social media service X. He surprised many people when he offered praise for Chalamet even before the project was released. He wrote, "Timmy's a brilliant actor, so I'm sure he's going to be completely believable as me. Or a younger me. Or some other me."[3]

Critics had many positive things to say about Chalamet's portrayal of Dylan. Peter Bradshaw of the

Chalamet had to learn how to ride a vintage 1964 Triumph Bonneville T100 motorcycle for the film.

Guardian said that he didn't buy Chalamet as Dylan until the actor began singing early in the film. He described the actor's portrayal of the musician as hypnotic.

Brian Tallerico, president of the Chicago Film Critics Association, thought that one of Chalamet's biggest accomplishments in the role was making moments in Dylan's life feel new and fresh to the audience. These events had taken place six decades earlier. And many people who saw the film were already familiar with much of Dylan's story.

Some critics disliked the liberties the movie took with that story. *New York Times* film critic Manohla Dargis was among them. She pointed out that the accuracy of the film isn't on point, but she called Chalamet the perfect actor to play the role.

> **"This is the movie I am the most proud of in my career."**[5]
>
> —Timothée Chalamet on *A Complete Unknown*, 2024

Many people who saw *A Complete Unknown* couldn't stop talking about Chalamet's performance. His fans wonder how he captures his characters so well in his work, but Chalamet considers this no one's business but his own, and he isn't afraid of saying so. He told Anderson Cooper that his acting secrets may not be as interesting as people think. He also added that if he shared them, they could overshadow his work, which is what he wants people to focus on.

IN PURSUIT OF GREATNESS

Released in December of 2024, *A Complete Unknown* was only a moderate success at the box office, bringing in $11 million its opening weekend.[4] While it wasn't a commercial hit, the film brought Chalamet several award nominations. His performance put him in the running for the Best Actor award at the Golden Globes, the Screen Actors Guild (SAG) Awards, and the Academy Awards. This second Academy Award nod made him the youngest person to be nominated for two Best Actor Oscars since James Dean in 1956.

Chalamet faced strong competition for all three awards. One of these contenders was Adrien Brody, who was nominated for the epic historical drama *The Brutalist*. In January 2025, Brody took home the Best Actor prize at the Golden Globes. The winners at this annual awards ceremony are chosen by the Hollywood Foreign Press Association, which is made up of journalists.

The SAG Awards, on the other hand, are voted on by members of the Screen Actors Guild, which includes many of the same people who vote for the Academy Award winners. For this reason, many people see a SAG Award win as a hint about who is most likely to win the Oscar.

When Chalamet won the SAG Award in late February, he said he wasn't expecting the honor. He told the audience that his goal in acting was to pursue greatness. He made it clear that he didn't think his win meant he had

LOOK-ALIKE CONTEST

On October 27, 2024, hundreds of Timothée Chalamet fans descended on Washington Square Park in New York City to participate in a Chalamet look-alike contest. Many of them were dressed as characters their favorite star had played in recent movies, including Willy Wonka and *Dune*'s Paul Atreides. Contestants were floored when Chalamet himself showed up at the event. In the end, 21-year-old Miles Mitchell, who was dressed as Wonka, won the competition, taking home a trophy and the $50 prize.[6]

Chalamet celebrated his SAG Award for *A Complete Unknown* with his mother, Nicole Flender, on February 23, 2025, in Los Angeles.

accomplished that goal yet, but he described it as a little more fuel for getting there.

The Oscar ceremony took place one week later. Chalamet attended the event with Kylie Jenner, his mother, and his sister. When he walked the red carpet, the press had a surprise for him. *Access Hollywood* showed him a message from his high school drama teacher, Harry Shifman. In a recording, Shifman spoke of Chalamet's wit, talent, and grace and encouraged him to take in the recognition of his artistry. Chalamet said the message meant a great deal to him.

Although Brody ended up winning the Oscar, Chalamet has solidified himself as a true artist among his fellow actors. Many of them expect to see his name among future Oscar nominees. With goals of telling good stories and portraying his characters as genuinely as possible, Chalamet has arguably already become one of the greatest actors of his time.

ESSENTIAL FACTS

Full Name: Timothée Hal Chalamet

Date of Birth: December 27, 1995

Place of Birth: New York City

Parents: Marc Chalamet and Nicole Flender

Education: Fiorello H. LaGuardia High School of Music & Art and Performing Arts

RISE TO STARDOM

- Chalamet's rise to fame began with his role as Elio Perlman in the 2017 film *Call Me by Your Name*.
- Chalamet's performance in *Call Me by Your Name* brought him his first Academy Award nomination at the age of 22.
- Chalamet faced challenges getting parts in mainstream movies, but he continued playing roles in indie films, including *Hot Summer Nights* and *Beautiful Boy*.
- The parts Chalamet played in indie movies led him to broader success in some of the most popular films of the 2020s.

CAREER HIGHLIGHTS

- Chalamet has been nominated for multiple acting awards since the start of his career.
- In 2025, Chalamet won the Screen Actors Guild Award for Best Actor for his performance of real-life folk singer Bob Dylan in *A Complete Unknown*.
- Chalamet's movies often top the box office, grossing hundreds of millions of dollars.

MAJOR FILMS

- *Call Me by Your Name* (2017)
- *Dune: Part One* (2021)
- *Wonka* (2023)
- *Dune: Part Two* (2024)
- *A Complete Unknown* (2024)
- *Dune: Part Three* (2026)

QUOTE

"The feeling of gratitude I have at the moment has less to do with individual achievement and more with the appreciation for the artists past honored in this category and all of the nominees of this year."

—Timothée Chalamet on his Oscar nomination for *Call Me by Your Name*

GLOSSARY

agent

A person who represents an actress or actor and is in charge of getting them auditions for parts.

antagonist

A character who presents conflict in a story.

biopic

A biographical movie.

contemporary

Occurring in the present period; current.

debut

The first time an actor, musician, or artist releases a product, such as an album.

ensemble

A group of performers who work together in a production.

gross

To earn income.

methamphetamine

A powerful and highly addictive stimulant drug.

monologue

A long speech often given at the beginning of a ceremony; also, a dramatic speech given by a single actor.

pandemic

An outbreak of disease over a large area.

paparazzi
Photographers who take photos of celebrities and sell them to the media.

phonetically
Expressed or understood through sounds rather than spelling.

prestigious
Honored or highly praised.

quarantine
A state or period of isolation, often to prevent the spread of a disease.

red carpet
An event before an awards show where performers or celebrities show up in gorgeous attire, get photographed, and do interviews.

sacrilegious
Showing blatant disrespect for a person or thing typically honored.

satirical
Done in a way that seems serious but is actually expressing ridicule.

versatility
The ability to perform in a wide range of ways.

vulnerability
An openness that leaves one at risk of being hurt physically or emotionally.

ADDITIONAL RESOURCES

SELECTED BIBLIOGRAPHY

Chi, Paul. "Timothée Chalamet Says *Wonka* Was His Most Challenging Role Yet." *Vanity Fair*, 11 Dec. 2023, vanityfair.com. Accessed 13 June 2025.

Cooper, Anderson, et al. "Timothée Chalamet Knew Almost Nothing about Bob Dylan. Here's How He Studied Him for *A Complete Unknown*." *CBS News*, 16 Feb. 2025, cbsnews.com. Accessed 13 June 2025.

Hirschberg, Lynn. "Timothée Chalamet and Denis Villeneuve Enter a 'Deep Dream State.'" *W Magazine*, 12 Feb. 2025, wmagazine.com. Accessed 13 June 2025.

FURTHER READINGS

Murray, Laura K. *Making Movies*. Abdo, 2024.

Pounder, Sibéal. *Wonka*. Viking, 2023.

Sonneborn, Liz. *Zendaya*. Abdo, 2026.

ONLINE RESOURCES

To learn more about Timothée Chalamet, please visit **abdobooklinks.com** or scan this QR code. These links are routinely monitored and updated to provide the most current information available.

MORE INFORMATION

For more information on this subject, contact or visit the following organizations:

ACADEMY MUSEUM OF MOTION PICTURES

6067 Wilshire Blvd.
Los Angeles, CA 90036
academymuseum.org/en

The Academy Museum of Motion Pictures is the largest museum in the United States devoted to the art and science of moviemaking. It features film screenings and interactive displays about many of the world's greatest movies.

BOB DYLAN CENTER

116 E. Reconciliation Way
Tulsa, OK 74103
bobdylancenter.com

The Bob Dylan Center in Tulsa, Oklahoma, features exhibits about one of the most influential American singer-songwriters and the artists he has inspired. The museum includes more than 100,000 items from throughout Dylan's career, such as song notebooks, photographs, and musical instruments.

WARNER BROS. STUDIO TOUR HOLLYWOOD

3400 Warner Blvd.
Burbank, CA 91505
wbstudiotour.com

Warner Bros. Studio Tour Hollywood offers tours of Warner Bros. film studios. Guests can also explore the WB Archive Museum, which features props, costumes, and photographs from movies such as Timothée Chalamet's *Dune* franchise.

SOURCE NOTES

CHAPTER 1. A NIGHT TO REMEMBER

1. "Timothée Chalamet | Oscars 2018." *YouTube*, uploaded by N, 5 Mar. 2018, youtube.com. Accessed 13 June 2025.

2. "Oscar Nominee Timothée Chalamet on 'Call Me by Your Name.'" *ABC News*, 26 Jan. 2018, abcnews.go.com. Accessed 30 June 2025.

3. Ale Russian. "Gary Oldman Has Sweet Words of Encouragement for Timothée Chalamet." *People*, 5 Mar. 2018, people.com. Accessed 13 June 2025.

4. "Timothée Chalamet on 'Call Me by Your Name.'"

5. Sandy Kenyon. "Going for Gold: The Stars of 'Call Me By Your Name.'" *ABC*, 22 Feb. 2018, abc11.com. Accessed 13 June 2025.

CHAPTER 2. CREATIVE BEGINNINGS

1. Ree Hines. "All about Timothée Chalamet's Parents." *Today*, 24 Dec. 2024, today.com. Accessed 30 June 2025.

2. Ariana Quihuiz. "All about Timothée Chalamet's Parents, Marc Chalamet and Nicole Flender." *People*, 23 Apr. 2025, people.com. Accessed 30 June 2025.

3. Quihuiz, "All about Timothée Chalamet's Parents."

4. Joanna Tweedy. "How Manhattan Plaza Has Housed Some Very Famous Residents." *Daily Mail*, 2 Mar. 2025, dailymail.co.uk. Accessed 30 June 2025.

5. Olivia Singh. "Timothée Chalamet's First Acting Role Was on 'Law & Order'—and Ellen DeGeneres Dug Up the Video." *Business Insider*, 11 Jan. 2019, businessinsider.com. Accessed 13 June 2025.

6. Josh Duboff. "Meet Timothée Chalamet and Ansel Elgort's High-School Drama Teacher, Mr. Shifman." *Vanity Fair*, 19 Jan. 2018, vanityfair.com. Accessed 13 June 2025.

CHAPTER 3. A STAR IN THE MAKING

1. "How Timothée Chalamet's Drama Teacher Helped Him Change His Life." *YouTube*, uploaded by *60 Minutes*, 16 Feb. 2025, youtube.com. Accessed 30 June 2025.

2. Josh Duboff. "Meet Timothée Chalamet and Ansel Elgort's High-School Drama Teacher, Mr. Shifman." *Vanity Fair*, 19 Jan. 2018, vanityfair.com. Accessed 13 June 2025.

3. Greg Evans. "Timothée Chalamet Shares 'Humiliating' High School Talent Show Audition." *Independent*, 17 Feb. 2025, independent.co.uk. Accessed 13 June 2025.

4. "How Timothée Chalamet's Drama Teacher Helped Him Change His Life."

5. Angela Barbuti. "Timothée Chalamet Was Voted 'Most Likely to Become Famous' in 8th Grade—Now He's Up for an Oscar." *New York Post*, 1 Mar. 2025, nypost.com. Accessed 13 June 2025.

6. Alex Cranz. "Timothée Chalamet Used to Mod Xbox 360 Controllers." *Verge*, 27 Oct. 2021, theverge.com. Accessed 13 June 2025.

7. Anna Kerrigan. "A 17-Year-Old Beanstalk from a Wholesome '70s Family Is Eager to Go Far Out." *New York Times*, 17 Aug. 2011, nytimes.com. 13 June 2025.

8. Duboff, "Meet Timothée Chalamet."

CHAPTER 4. PROGRESS AND CHALLENGES

1. Sam Moore. "Watch Timothée Chalamet's Excellent Impression of Matthew McConaughey." *NME*, 3 Mar. 2018, nme.com. Accessed 30 June 2025.

2. Maura Hohman. "Timothée Chalamet Admits He 'Wept' After Seeing 'Interstellar' Because His Part Was So Small." *People*, 4 Dec. 2018, people.com. Accessed 30 June 2025.

3. "Nardwuar vs. Timothée Chalamet." *YouTube*, uploaded by NardwuarServiette, 25 Dec. 2024, youtube.com. Accessed 13 June 2025.

4. Ariana Quihuiz. "All about Timothée Chalamet's Parents, Marc Chalamet and Nicole Flender." *People*, 23 Apr. 2025, people.com. Accessed 30 June 2025.

5. "Young Hollywood Star Timothée Chalamet on 'Homeland.'" *Teen Vogue*, 1 Oct. 2014, teenvogue.com. Accessed 13 June 2025.

6. Matthew Jacobs. "They Discovered Timmy." *Vulture*, 4 Dec. 2023, vulture.com. Accessed 13 June 2025.

CHAPTER 5. THE YEAR THAT CHANGED HIS CAREER

1. "Oscars: The Nominees React." *Hollywood Reporter*, 23 Jan. 2018, hollywoodreporter.com. Accessed 13 June 2025.

2. Anna Menta. "Timothée Chalamet on 'Call Me By Your Name.'" *Newsweek*, 24 Nov. 2017, newsweek.com. Accessed 30 June 2025.

SOURCE NOTES

3. Abigail Thomas. "Timothée Chalamet Was the Only Actor to Audition for This Movie." *The Things*, 5 June 2023, thethings.com. Accessed 30 June 2025.

4. Thomas, "Chalamet the Only Actor to Audition."

5. "Hostiles." *Bomb Report*, 2017, bombreport.com. Accessed 13 June 2025.

6. Kate Bove. "Greta Gerwig's $79 Million Movie from 6 Years Ago Deserves the Same Love as Barbie." *Screen Rant*, 18 Dec. 2023, screenrant.com. Accessed 13 June 2025.

CHAPTER 6. SHOWING HIS RANGE

1. Lynn Hirschberg. "Timothée Chalamet in Conversation: A Raw, Honest Talk about Addiction, Recovery, and His Film *Beautiful Boy*." *W Magazine*, 17 Jan. 2019, wmagazine.com. Accessed 13 June 2025.

2. Hirschberg, "Timothée Chalamet in Conversation."

3. Kenneth Turan. "Review: Timothée Chalamet Might Be the Male Actor of His Generation, and 'Beautiful Boy' Is One Reason Why." *Los Angeles Times*, 11 Oct. 2018, latimes.com. Accessed 13 June 2025.

4. Jess Cohen. "Timothée Chalamet Recalls Shooting *Beautiful Boy* Scene Over 20 Times at 2019 Golden Globes." *E News*, 6 Jan. 2019, eonline.com. Accessed 13 June 2025.

5. Alexia Fernández. "'Little Women' Surpasses $100 Million at Worldwide Box Office as It Scores Six Oscar Nominations." *People*, 13 Jan. 2020, people.com. Accessed 13 June 2025.

6. Wade Sheridan. "Timothée Chalamet Says Little Women 'Gets at the Pursuit of Artistry.'" *United Press International*, 10 Dec. 2019, upi.com. Accessed 30 June 2025.

7. Rachel McRady. "Timothée Chalamet Shares His Genuine Reaction to the Viral Makeout Pics with Ex Lily-Rose Depp." *Entertainment Tonight*, 15 Oct. 2020, etonline.com. Accessed 30 June 2025.

CHAPTER 7. FROM INDIE FILMS TO BLOCKBUSTERS

1. "Dune: Part One." *Internet Movie Database*, n.d., imdb.com. Accessed 13 June 2025.

2. Scott Mendelson. "As 'Dune' Passes $400 Million, Can 'Dune Part Two' Rewrite Box Office History?" *Forbes*, 15 Feb. 2022, forbes.com. Accessed 13 June 2025.

CONTINUED. . .

3. "Wonka." *Box Office Mojo*, n.d., boxofficemojo.com. Accessed 13 June 2025.

4. Paul Chi. "Timothée Chalamet Says *Wonka* Was His Most Challenging Film Yet." *Vanity Fair*, 11 Dec. 2023, vanityfair.com. Accessed 13 June 2025.

5. Tatiana Siegal and Rebecca Rubin. "Hollywood's New A-List: Timothée Chalamet Gets Salary Boost after Box Office Hits." *Variety*, 13 Mar. 2024, variety.com. Accessed 13 June 2025.

6. Tom Shone. "The 90-Second Film That Earned Timothée Chalamet $35 Million—and Could Save Hollywood." *Telegraph*, 4 Aug. 2024, telegraph.co.uk. Accessed 13 June 2025.

7. Hashim Asraff. "Marvel and DC Need to Take Some Notes." *Internet Movie Database*, 21 Feb. 2024, imdb.com. Accessed 13 June 2025.

8. "Dune: Part Two." *Box Office Mojo*, n.d., boxofficemojo.com. Accessed 13 June 2025.

CHAPTER 8. LIKE A ROLLING STONE

1. Anderson Cooper, Aliza Chasan, Nicole Marks, and John Gallen. "Timothée Chalamet Knew Almost Nothing about Bob Dylan. Here's How He Studied Him for 'A Complete Unknown.'" *CBS News*, 16 Feb. 2025, cbsnews.com. Accessed 30 June 2025.

2. Bentley Maddox. "Why Timothée Chalamet Gained 20 Pounds to Play Bob Dylan in *A Complete Unknown*." *E News*, 28 Jan. 2025, eonline.com. Accessed 13 June 2025.

3. Maddox, "Why Timothée Chalamet Gained 20 Pounds."

4. Ethan Vlessing. "Timothée Chalamet Follows James Dean as Youngest Two-Time Oscar Best Actor Nominee." *Hollywood Reporter*, 23 Jan. 2025, hollywoodreporter.com. Accessed 13 June 2025.

5. "'I Was Just a Crazy Kid in High School . . .' Timothée Chalamet Opens Up on His Life in Hell's Kitchen." *Bang Showbiz*, 6 Jan. 2025, nz.news.yahoo.com. Accessed 13 June 2025.

6. "Timothée Chalamet Crashes His Own Lookalike Contest in NYC." *YouTube*, uploaded by Access Hollywood, 28 Oct. 2024, youtube.com. Accessed 13 June 2025.

INDEX

Academy Awards, 4–9, 10, 13, 50, 62, 84, 97, 98
Academy of Motion Pictures Arts and Sciences' Actor's Branch, 7

Baby Driver, 31
Bale, Christian, 54–57
Beautiful Boy, 12, 65–68, 88
Bones and All, 12, 82–83
Booker T. Washington Middle School, 25
British Academy of Film and Television Arts (BAFTA) Awards, 67
Brody, Adrien, 26, 97–99
Brolin, Josh, 77

Cabaret, 35
Call Me By Your Name, 4–9, 12, 24, 50–55, 59–60, 62, 64, 77, 81–82, 88, 92
Chalamet, Jean, 23
Chalamet, Marc, 14–16, 18, 41
Chalamet, Pauline, 17, 26, 69–70, 99
Chalamet, Roger, 23
Chastain, Jessica, 42
Columbia University, 22, 42–44
Complete Unknown, A, 13, 90–99
Cruise, Tom, 84

Dark Knight, The, 29
Day-Lewis, Daniel, 8
De Niro, Robert, 20
Dean, James, 47, 48, 67, 97
Death of a Salesman, 47
Depp, Johnny, 79
Depp, Lily-Rose, 64–65, 70–71
Dune (novel), 74, 78
Dune: Part One, 12, 74–78, 80, 93, 98
Dune: Part Two, 12, 84–86, 91, 93, 98
Dylan, Bob, 12–13, 88–96

Elgort, Ansel, 31

Fallon, Jimmy, 69
Fault in Our Stars, The, 31
Fiorello H. LaGuardia High School, 26–37
Flender, Hal, 21–22
Flender, Nicole, 4, 14, 16–18, 21, 26, 29, 99
4,000 Miles, 73
French Dispatch, The, 71–73, 77

Gerwig, Greta, 57–59, 68
Golden Globe Awards, 59, 67, 68, 87, 97–98
Guadagnino, Luca, 50–53, 78, 81–83

Hair, 17
Hall, Rebecca, 60–61
Hathaway, Anne, 42
Homeland, 36–37, 48, 59
Hostiles, 54–57
Hot Summer Nights, 49

Interstellar, 40–42, 44

Jenner, Kylie, 86–87, 98

Kaluuya, Daniel, 8
Keys, Alicia, 20
Kimmel, Jimmy, 6, 14
King, The, 11, 62–64, 70, 71

Lady Bird, 57–59, 64
Law & Order, 25
Ledger, Heath, 29
Leon, Lourdes, 30–31
Lithgow, John, 42
Little Women, 68–70, 71, 88

Manhattan Plaza, 18–20
McConaughey, Matthew, 40–42
McDormand, Frances, 72
Men, Women & Children, 38
Miss Stevens, 46–48
Mitchell-Lama Housing Program, 19
Momoa, Jason, 77
Murray, Bill, 72
Muyl, Alex, 23

New York University, 43
Newman, Griffin, 60–61

Oldman, Gary, 8, 13

Pattinson, Robert, 64
Pike, Rosamund, 54
Plemons, Jesse, 54
Prodigal Son, 48, 57, 88

Rainy Day in New York, A, 12, 60–61
Ronan, Saoirse, 57, 59, 69
Royal Pains, 35
Russell, Taylor, 82–83

Sandler, Adam, 40
Saturday Night Live, 10, 87
Screen Actors Guild (SAG) Award, 97, 98
Shifman, Harry, 26–28, 34, 37, 99
Simon, Paul, 48–49
Slava's Snowshow, 17
South by Southwest Film Festival, 47
Sweet Charity, 34

Talls, The, 33
Tonight Show, The, 69

van Groeningen, Felix, 68
Villeneuve, Denis, 74, 76, 78, 85

Washington, Denzel, 8
Wilder, Gene, 79–80
Williams, Tennessee, 20
Wonka, 12, 79–81, 87, 93, 98

Zendaya, 77, 78, 84

ABOUT THE AUTHOR

TAMMY GAGNE

Tammy Gagne is an author and editor with a passion for educational nonfiction. She has written hundreds of books for both adults and children. Residing in the beautiful state of Maine, she enjoys life with her husband, their son, and two rescue dogs. When not writing or editing, she is often brainstorming her next project. Some of her recent titles are about America's ethnic diversity and the physics that make flight possible. She hopes her books inspire and educate readers of all ages.